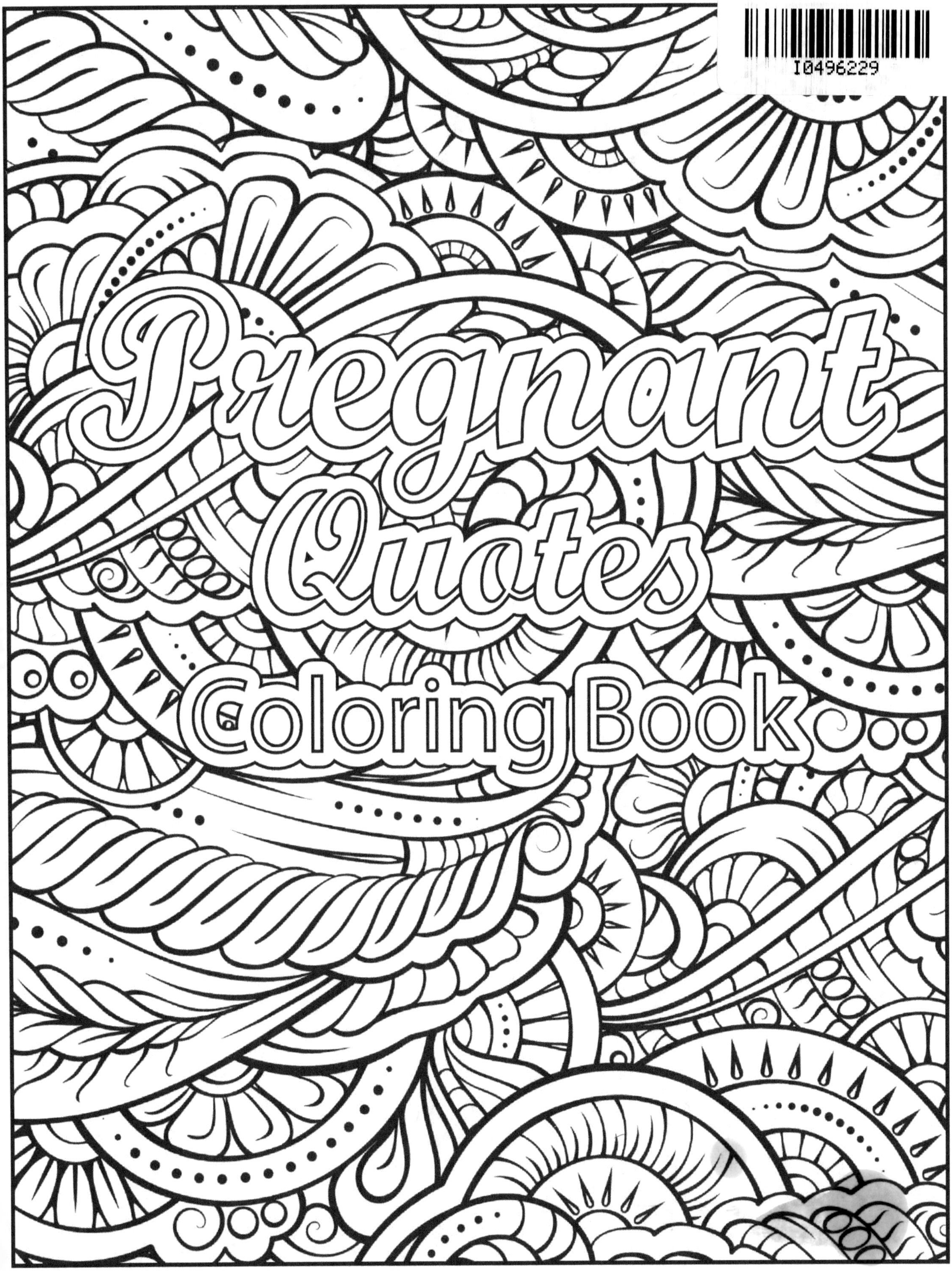
Pregnant
Quotes
Coloring Book

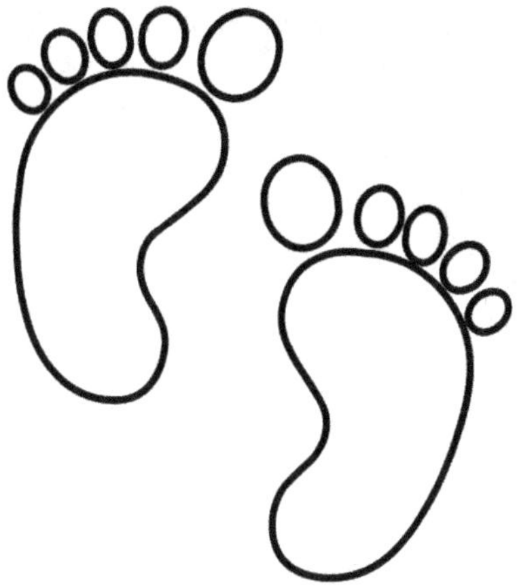

This book belongs to:

____

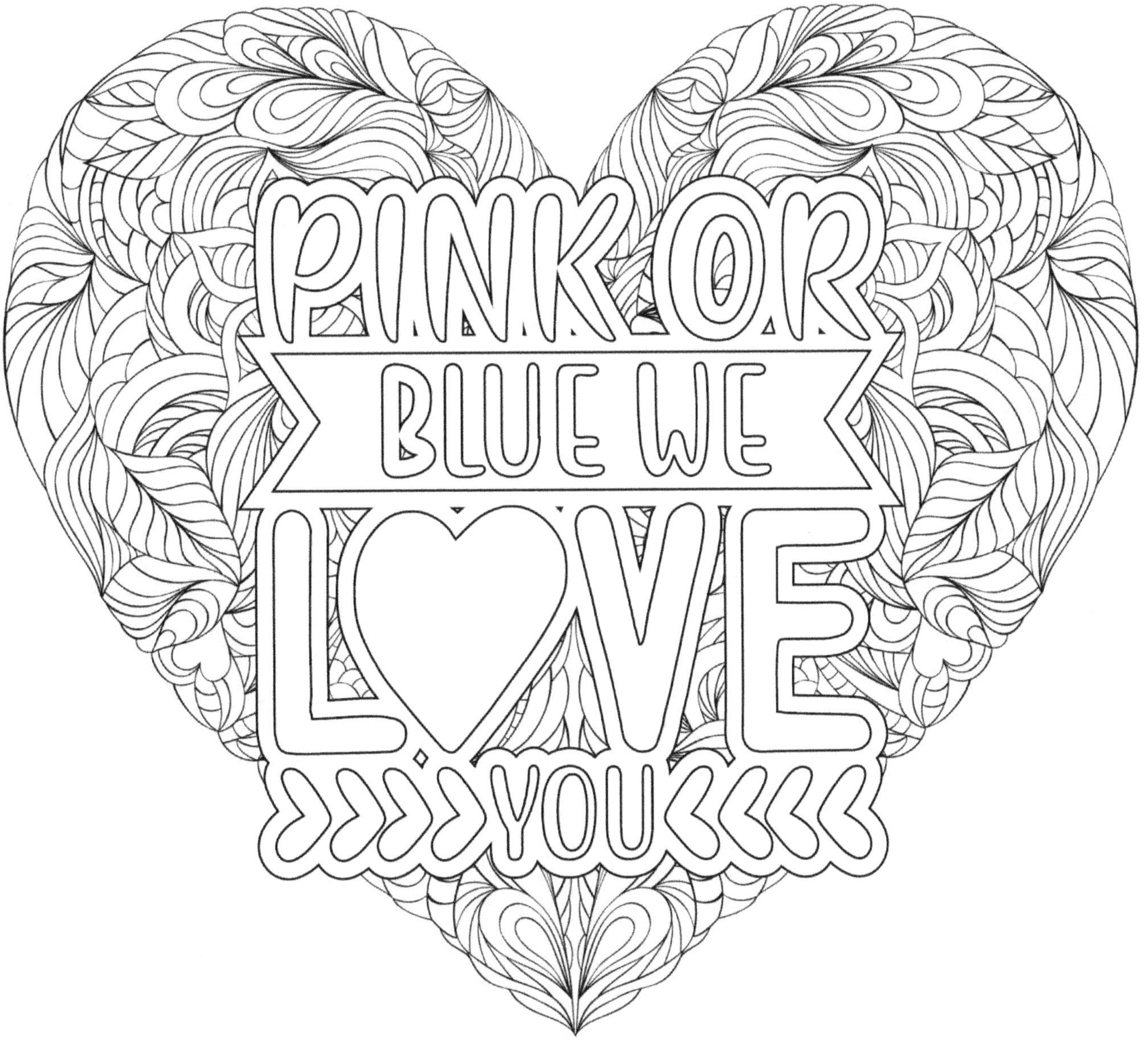
PINK OR
BLUE WE
LOVE
YOU

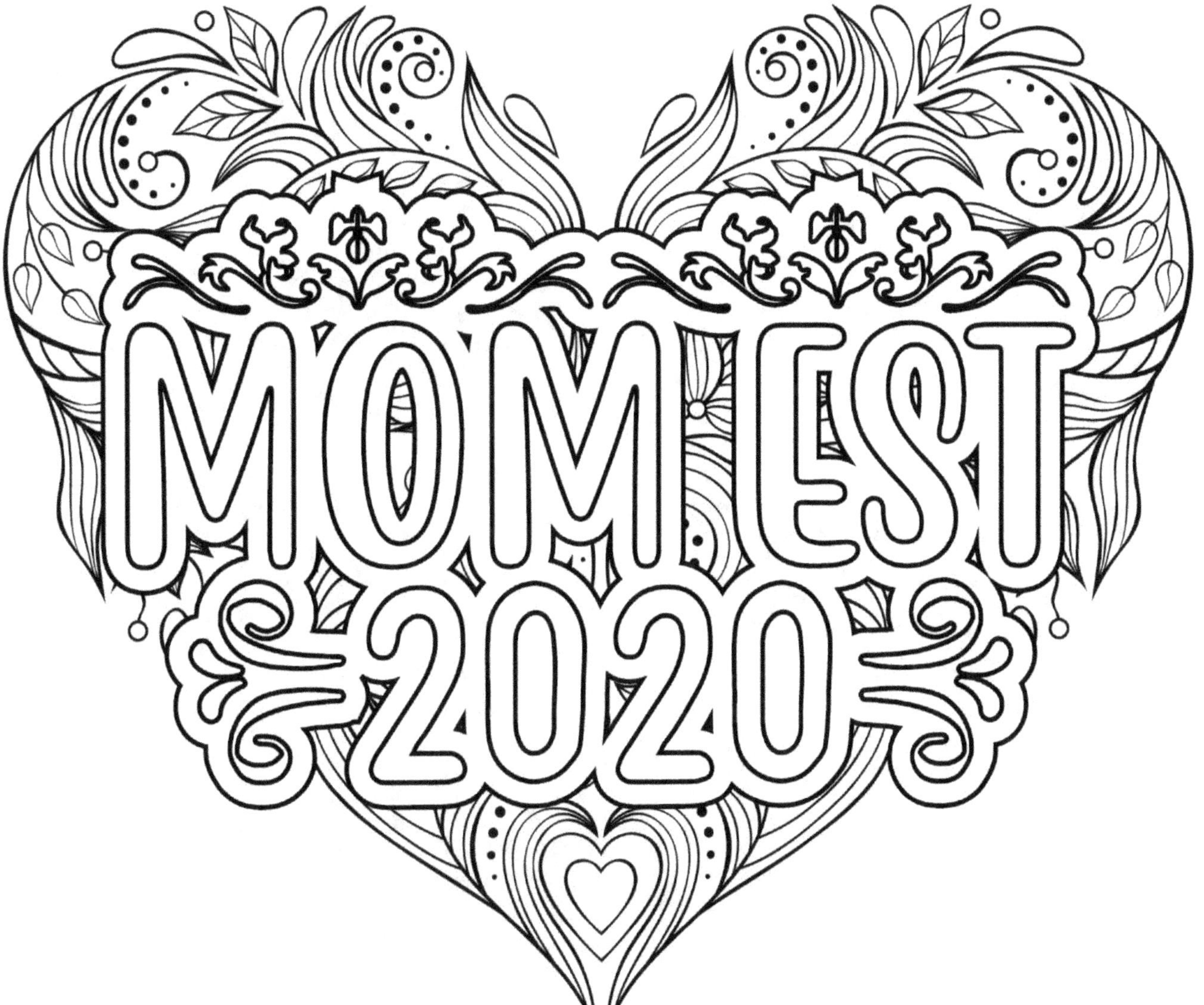
MOM EST
2020

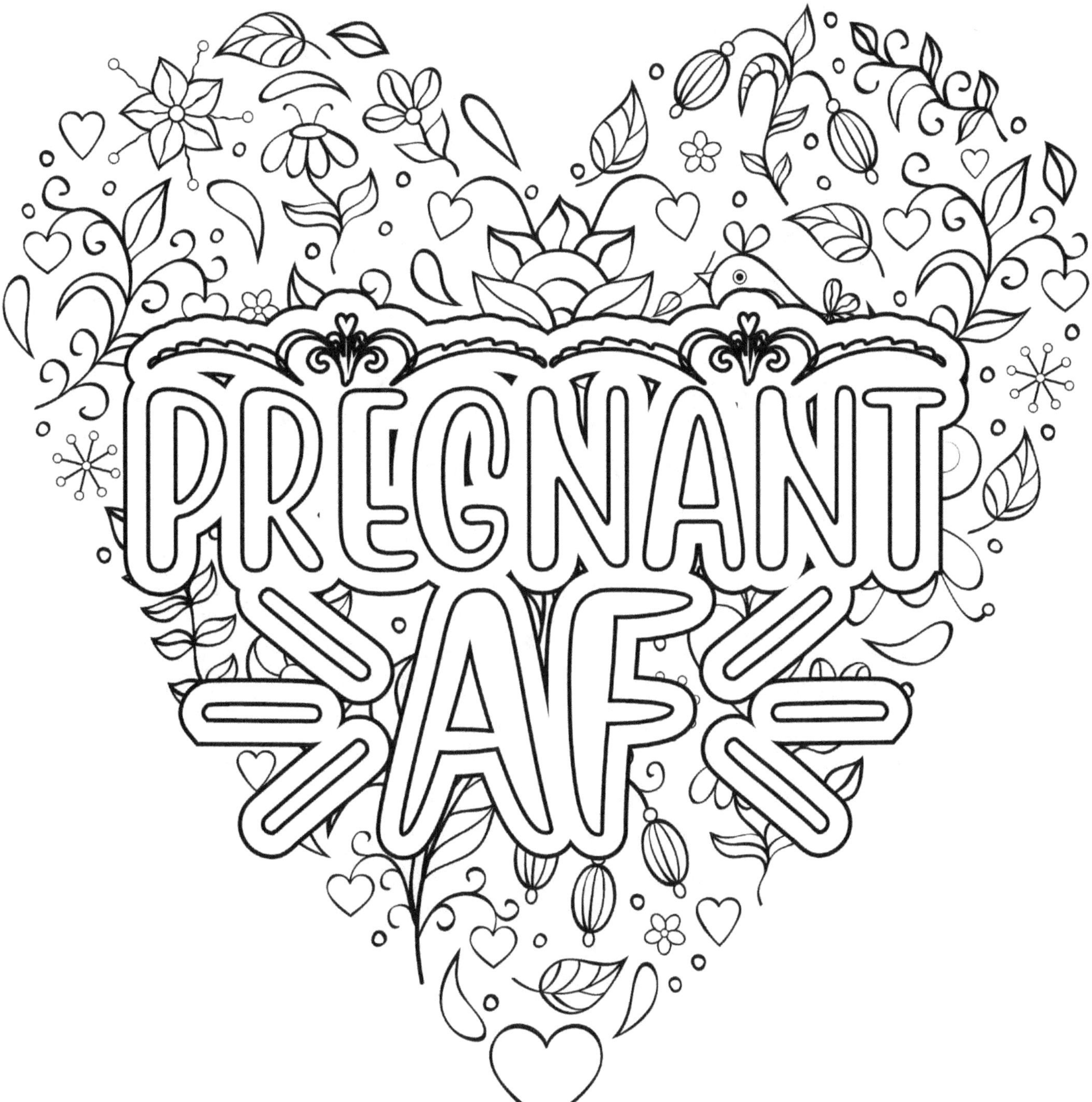
PREGNANT
AF

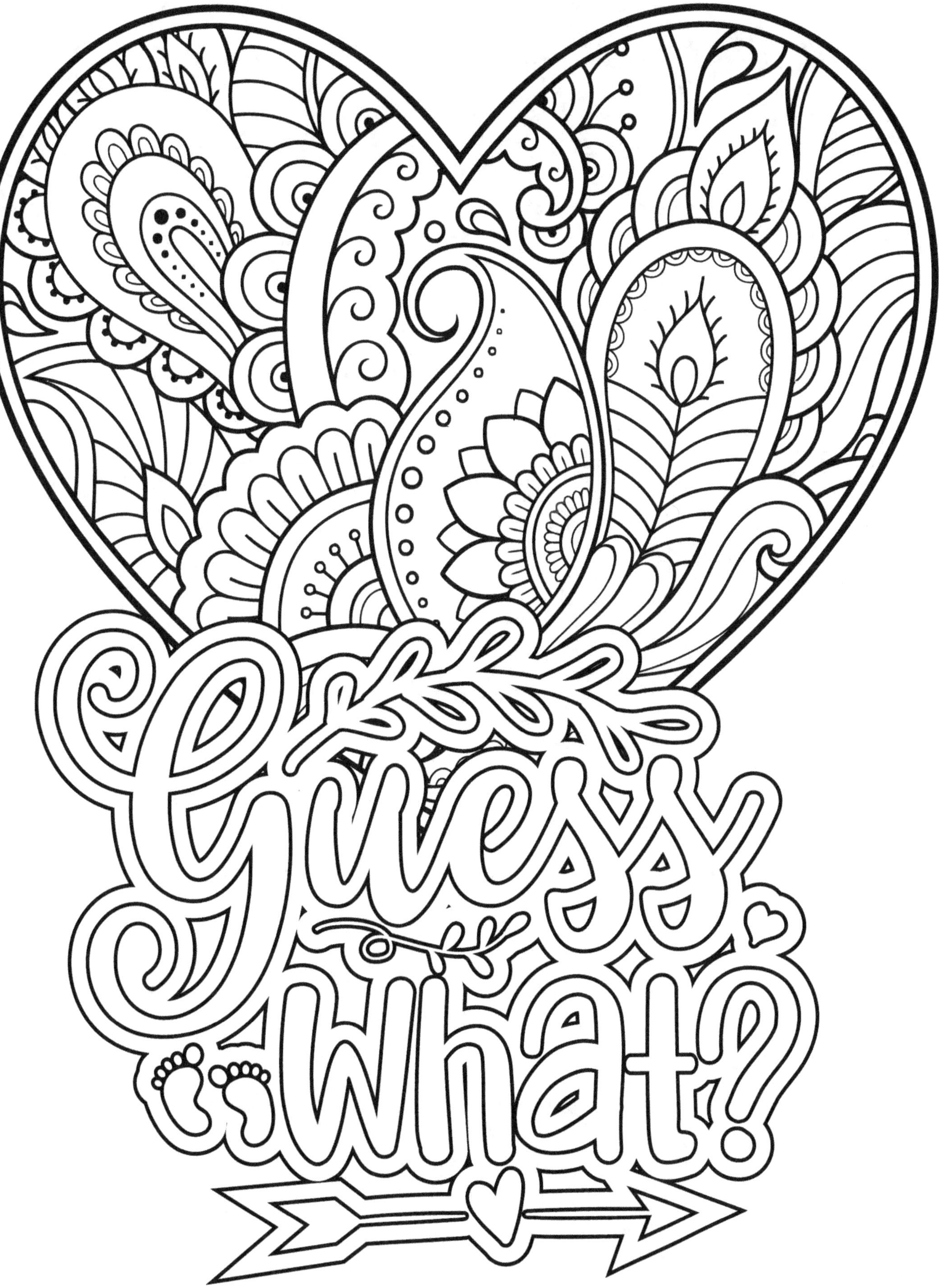
Guess What?

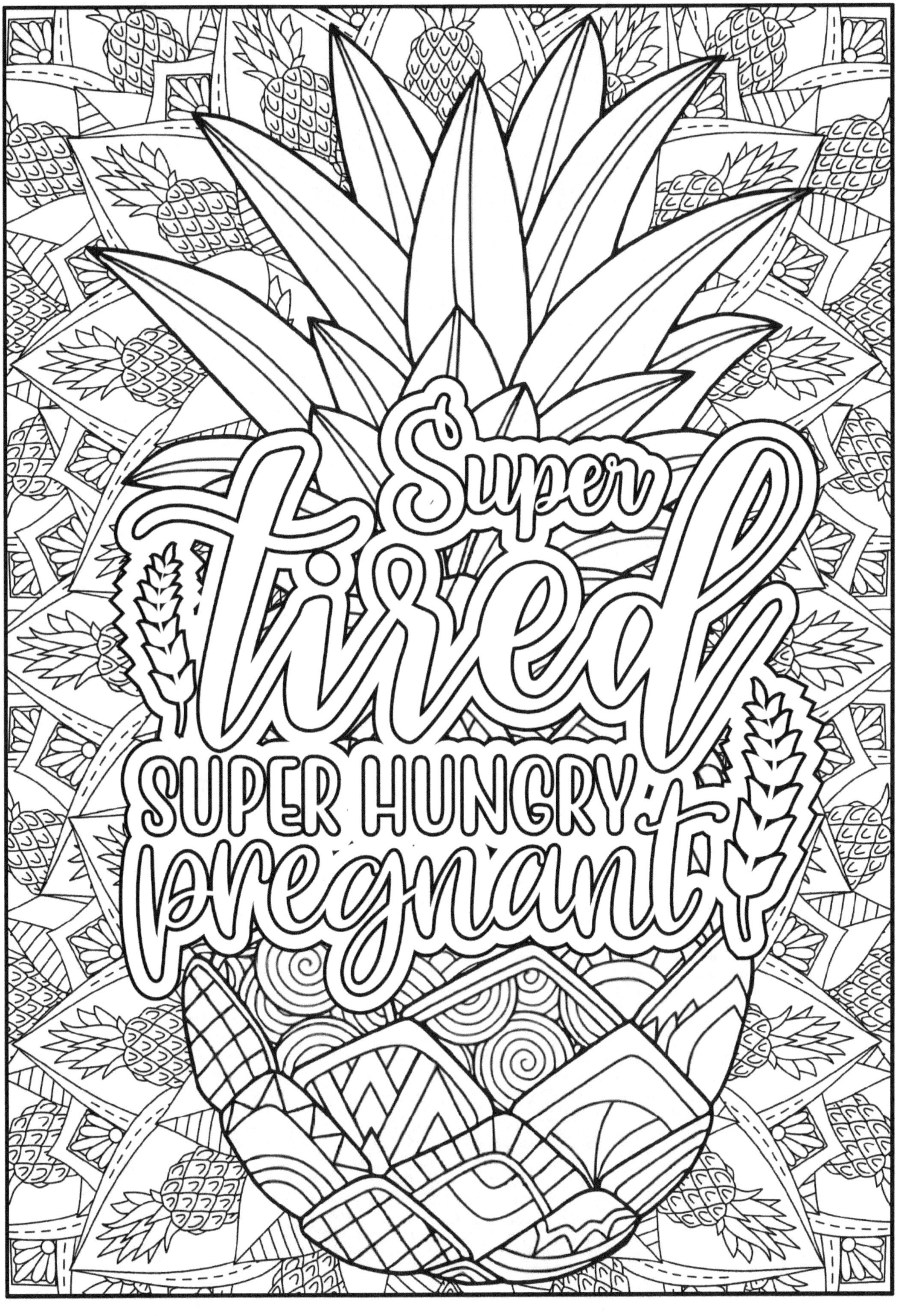
Super
tired
SUPER HUNGRY:
pregnant

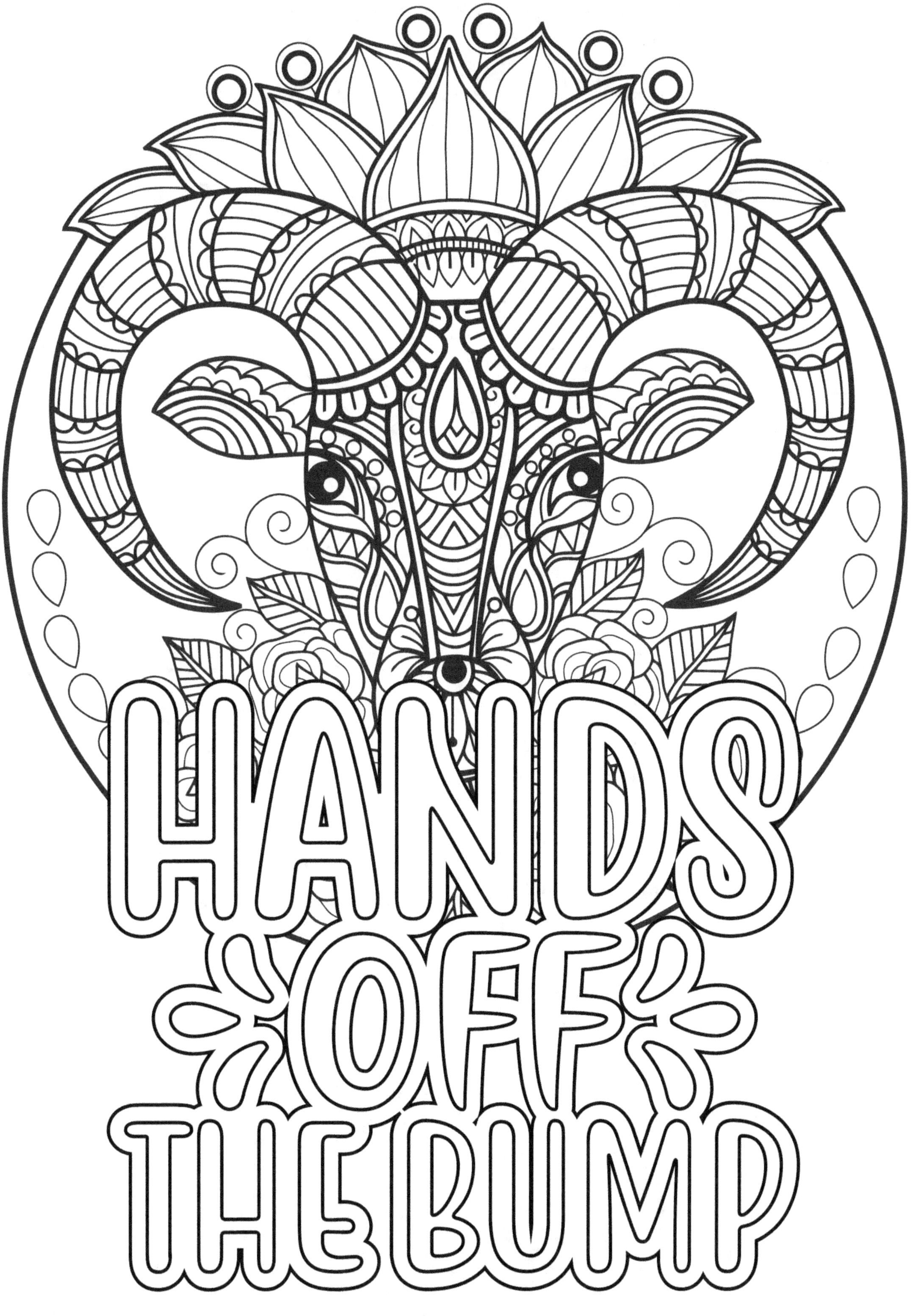
HANDS
OFF
THE BUMP

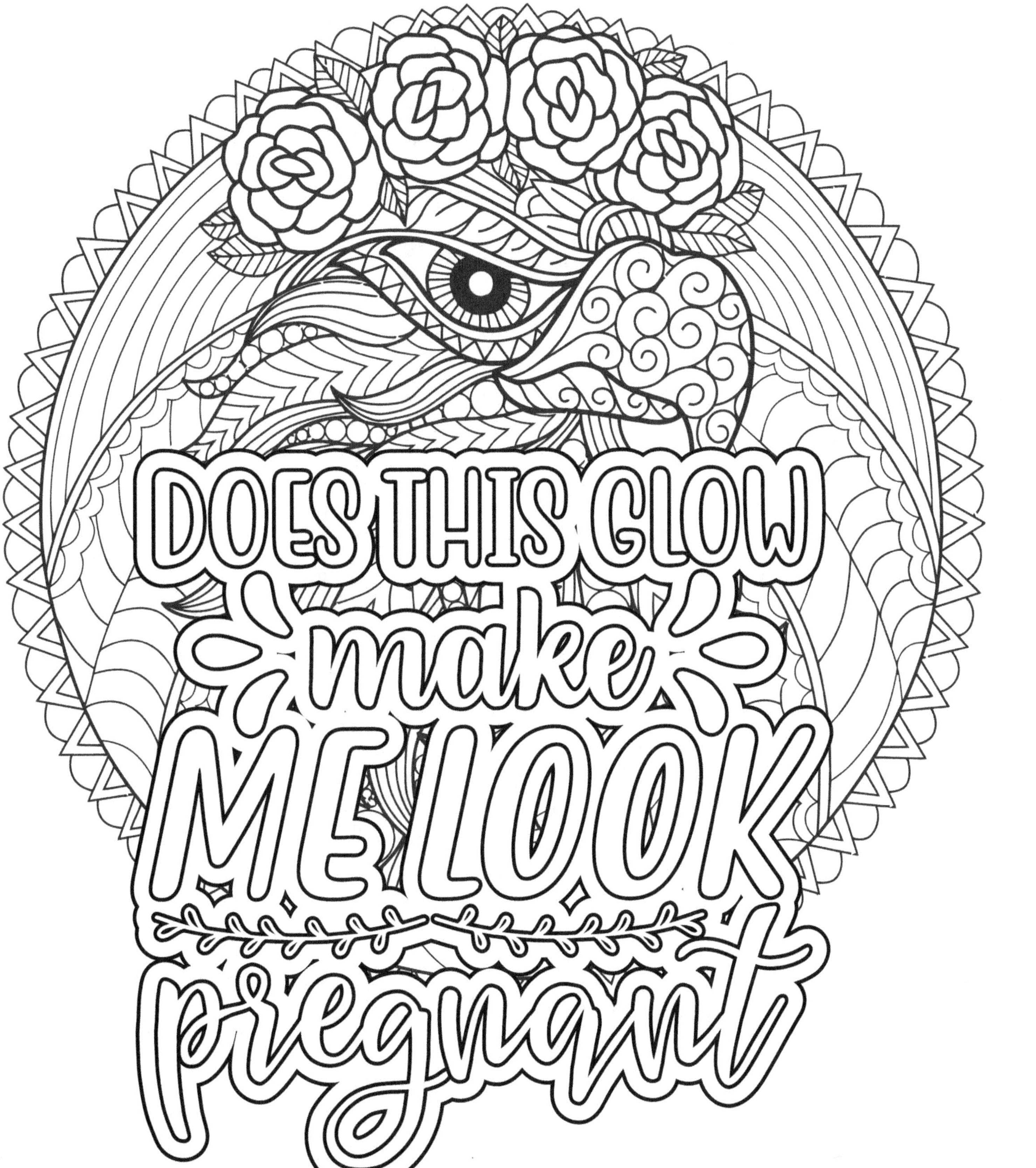
DOES THIS GLOW
make
ME LOOK
pregnant

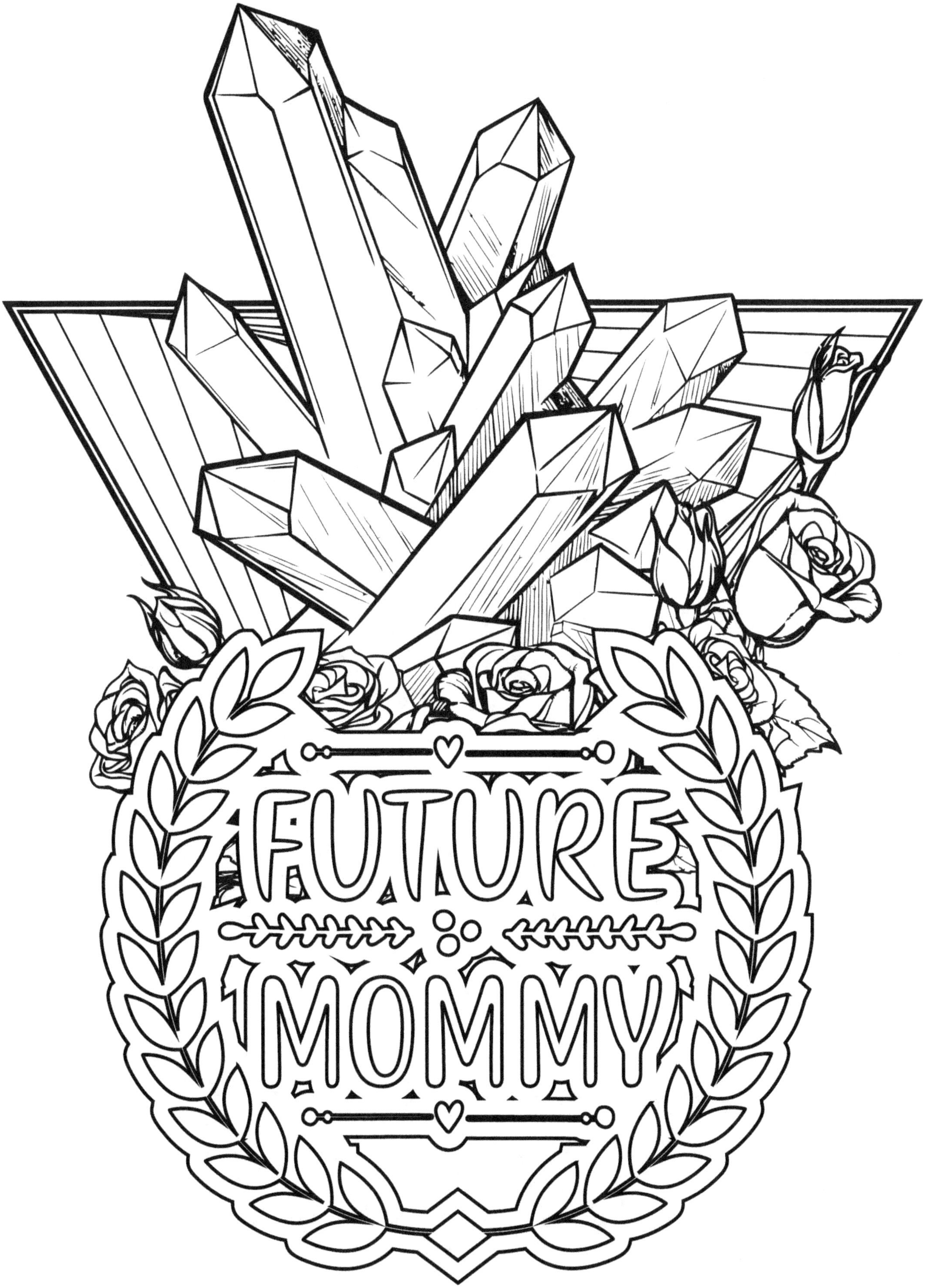
FUTURE
MOMMY

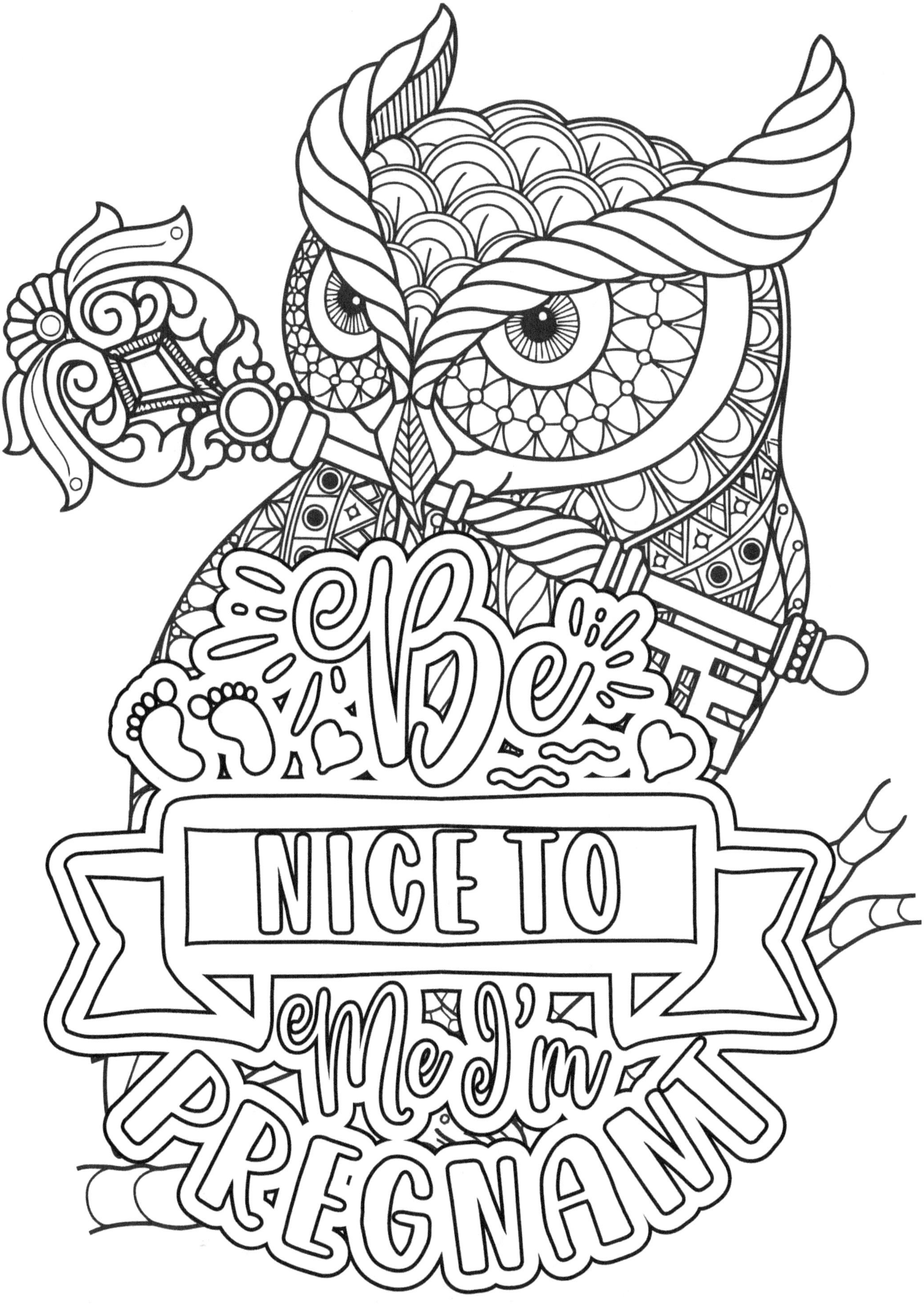
Be
NICE TO
Me I'm
PREGNANT

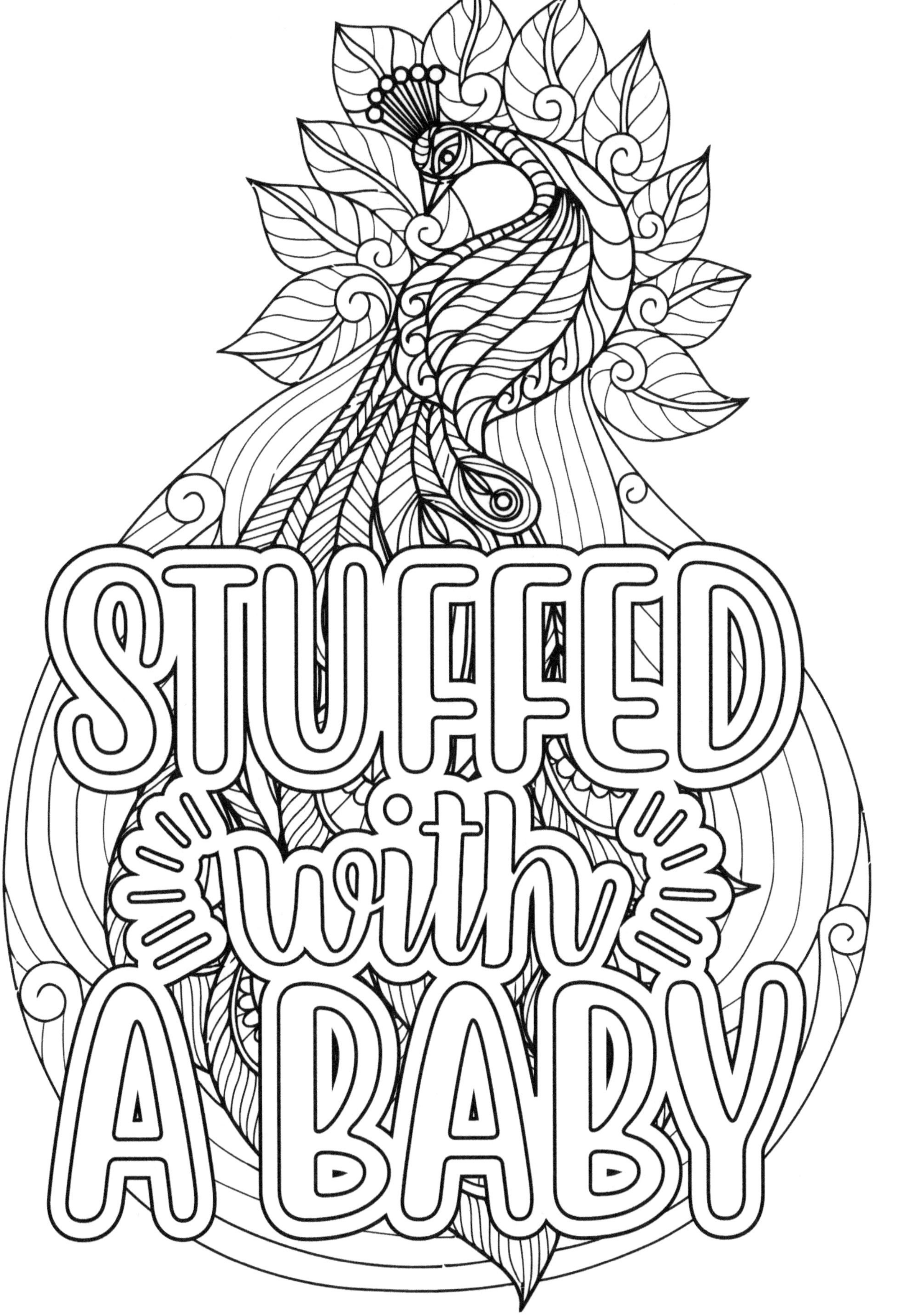
STUFFED
with
A BABY

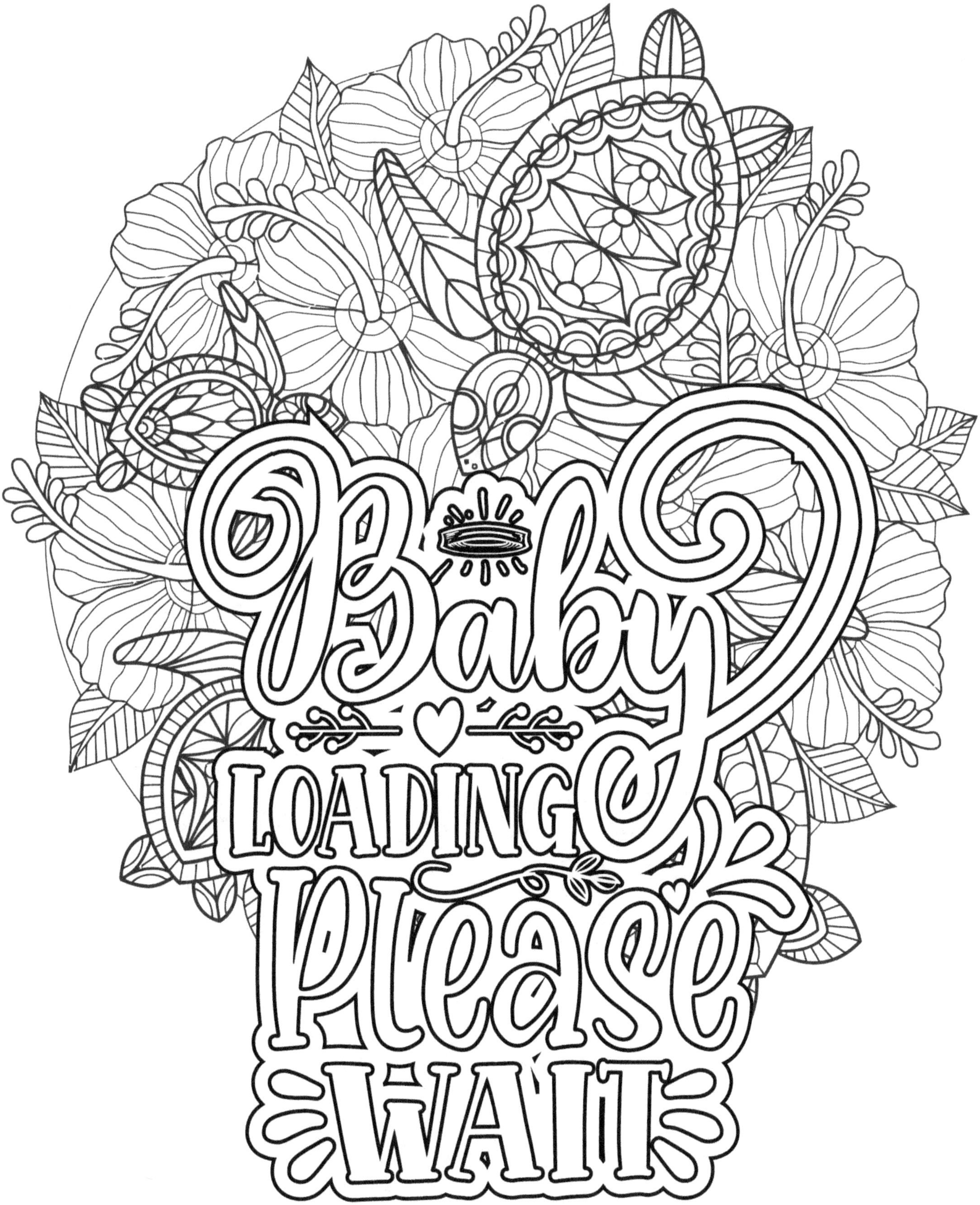
Baby
LOADING
Please
WAIT

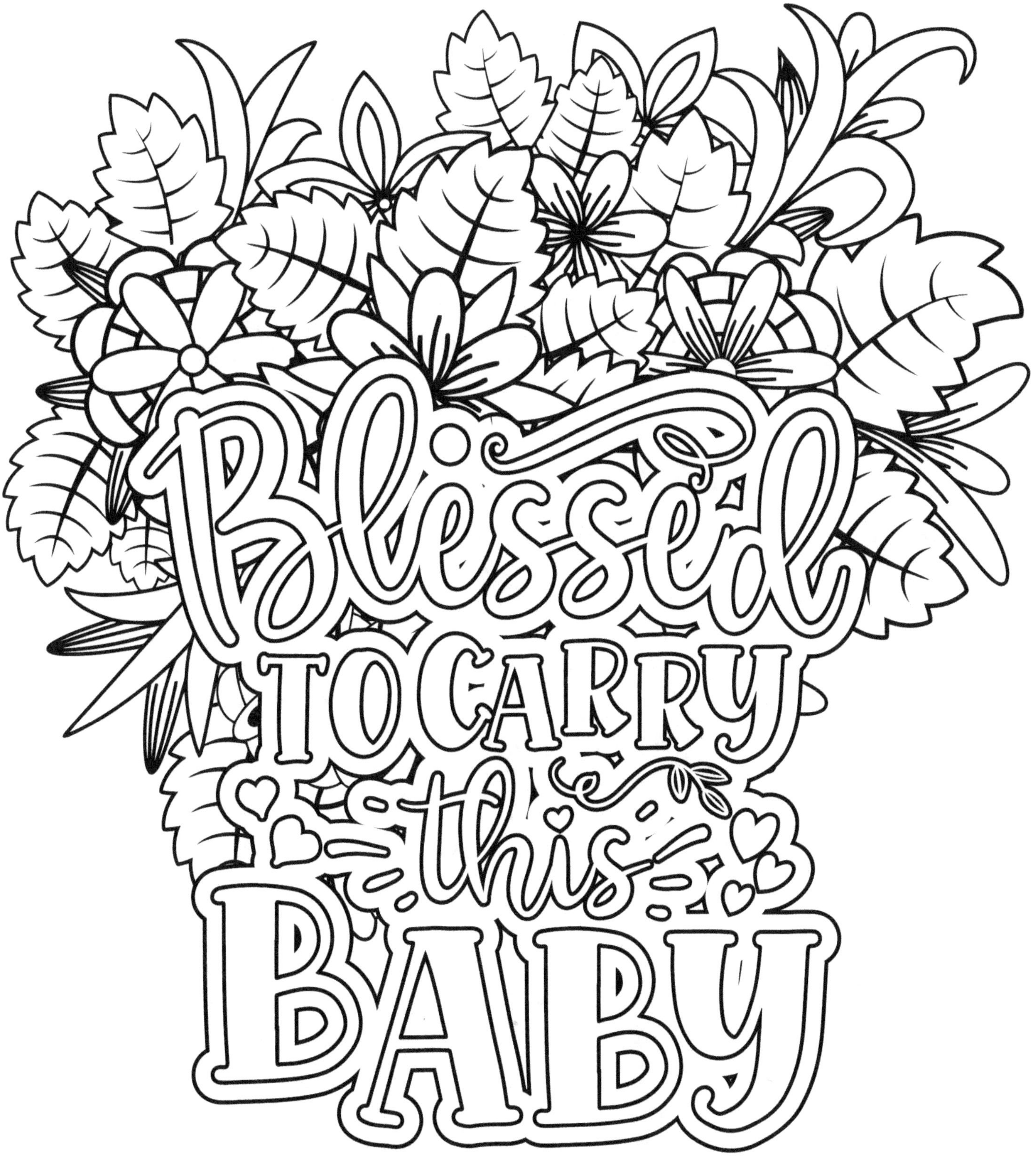
Blessed
TO CARRY
this
BABY

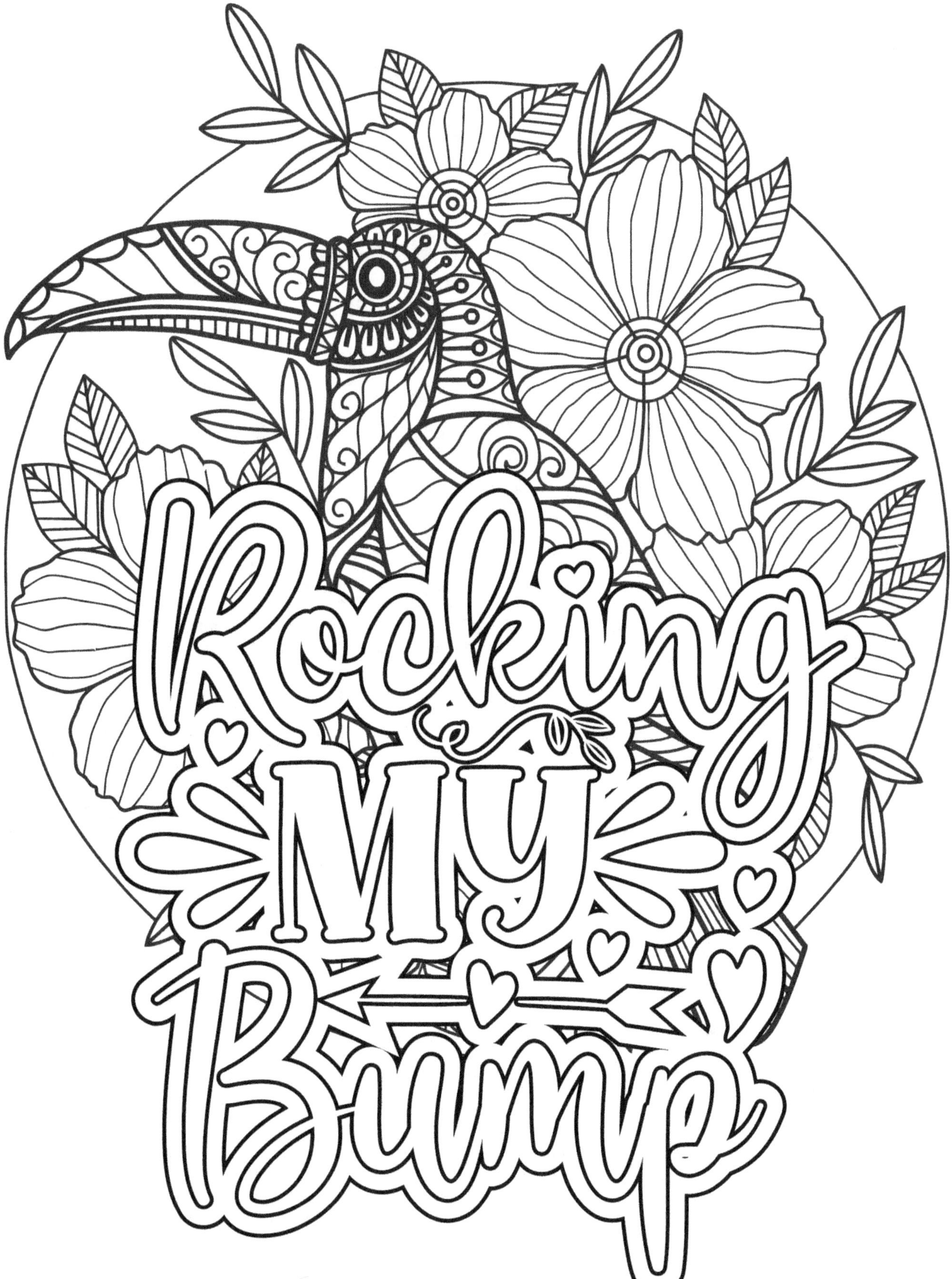
Rocking
MY
Bump

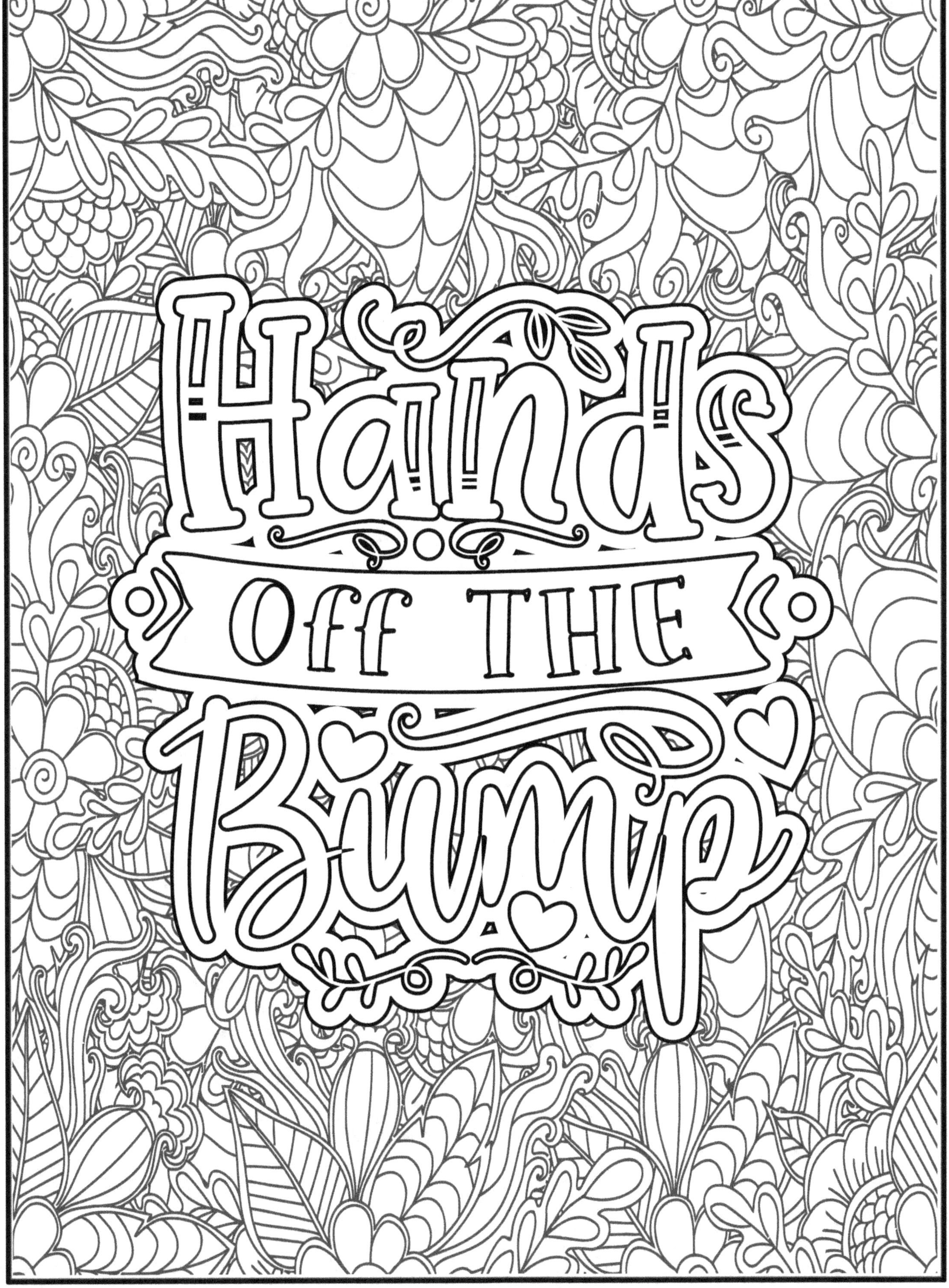
Hands
OFF THE
Bump

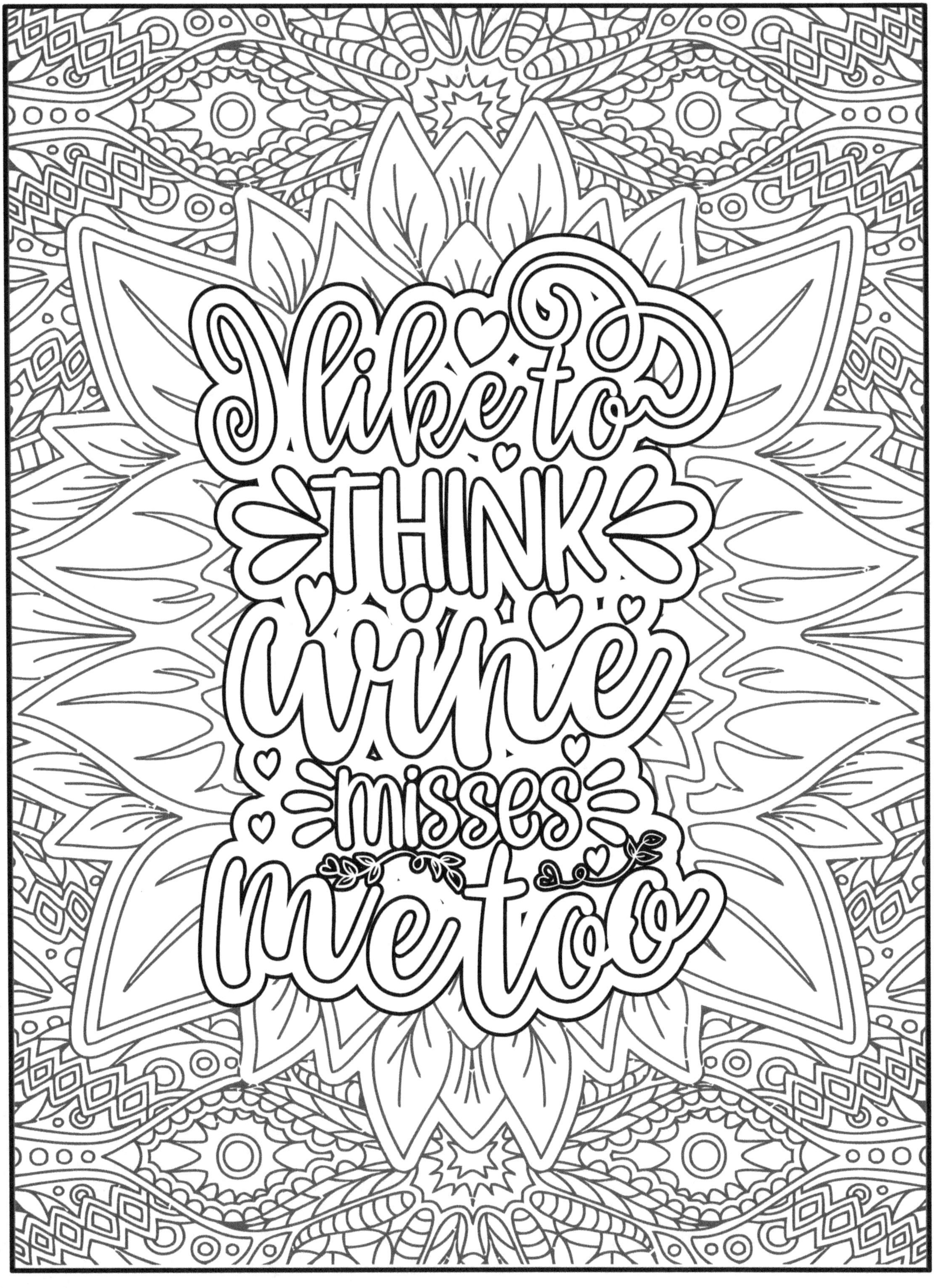
I like to
THINK
wine
misses
me too

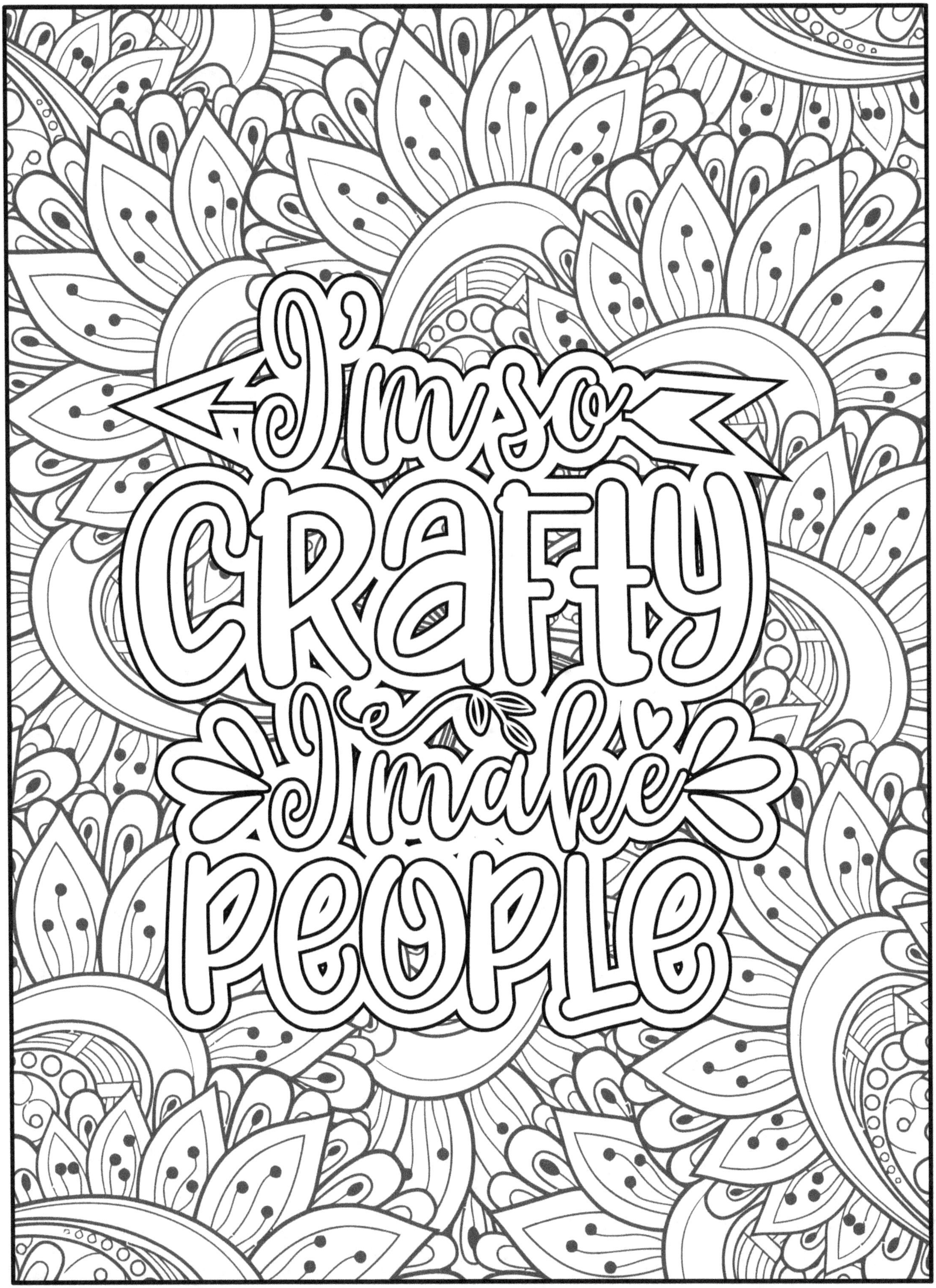
I'm so
CRAFTY
I make
PEOPLE

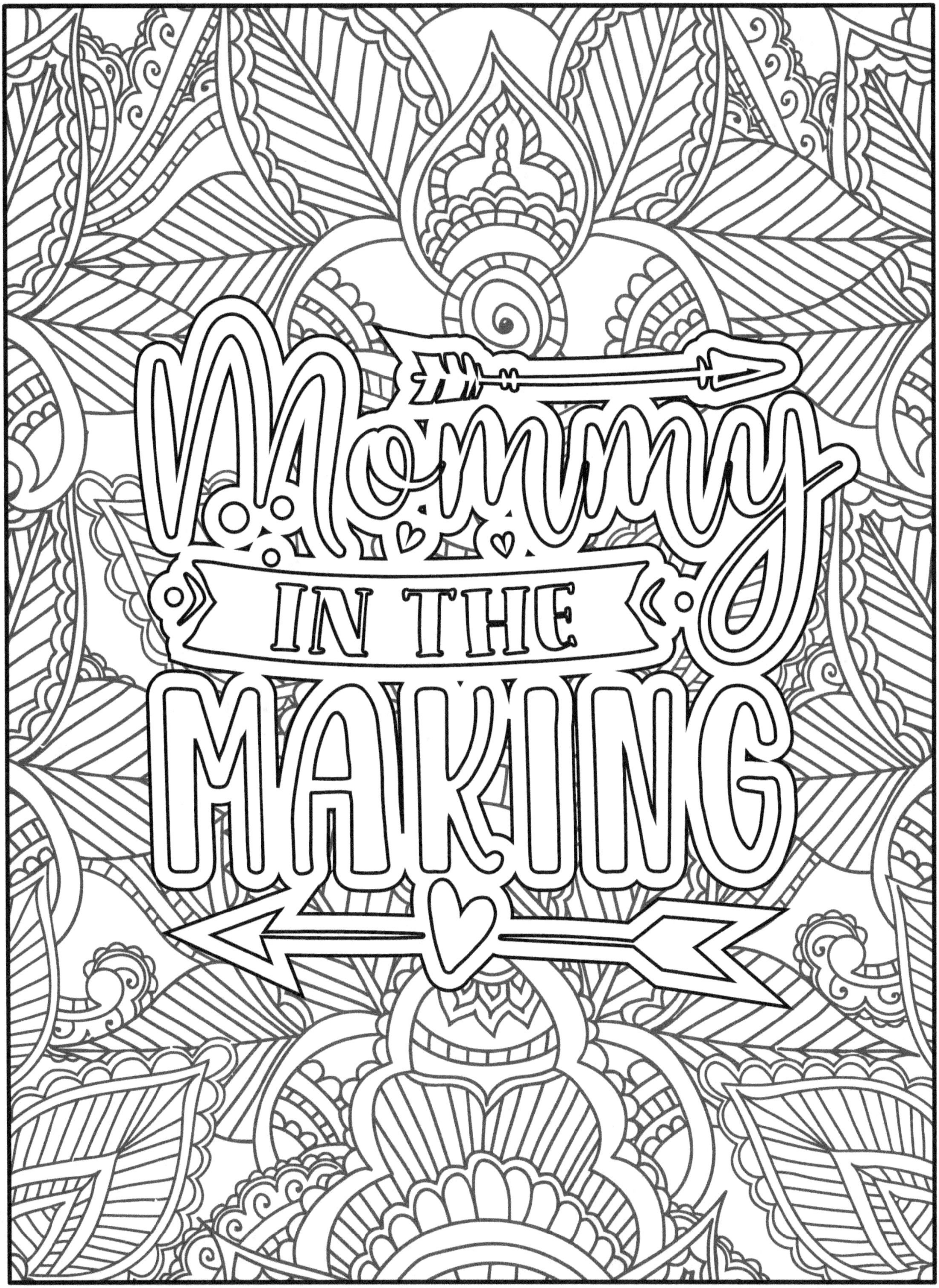
Mommy
IN THE
MAKING

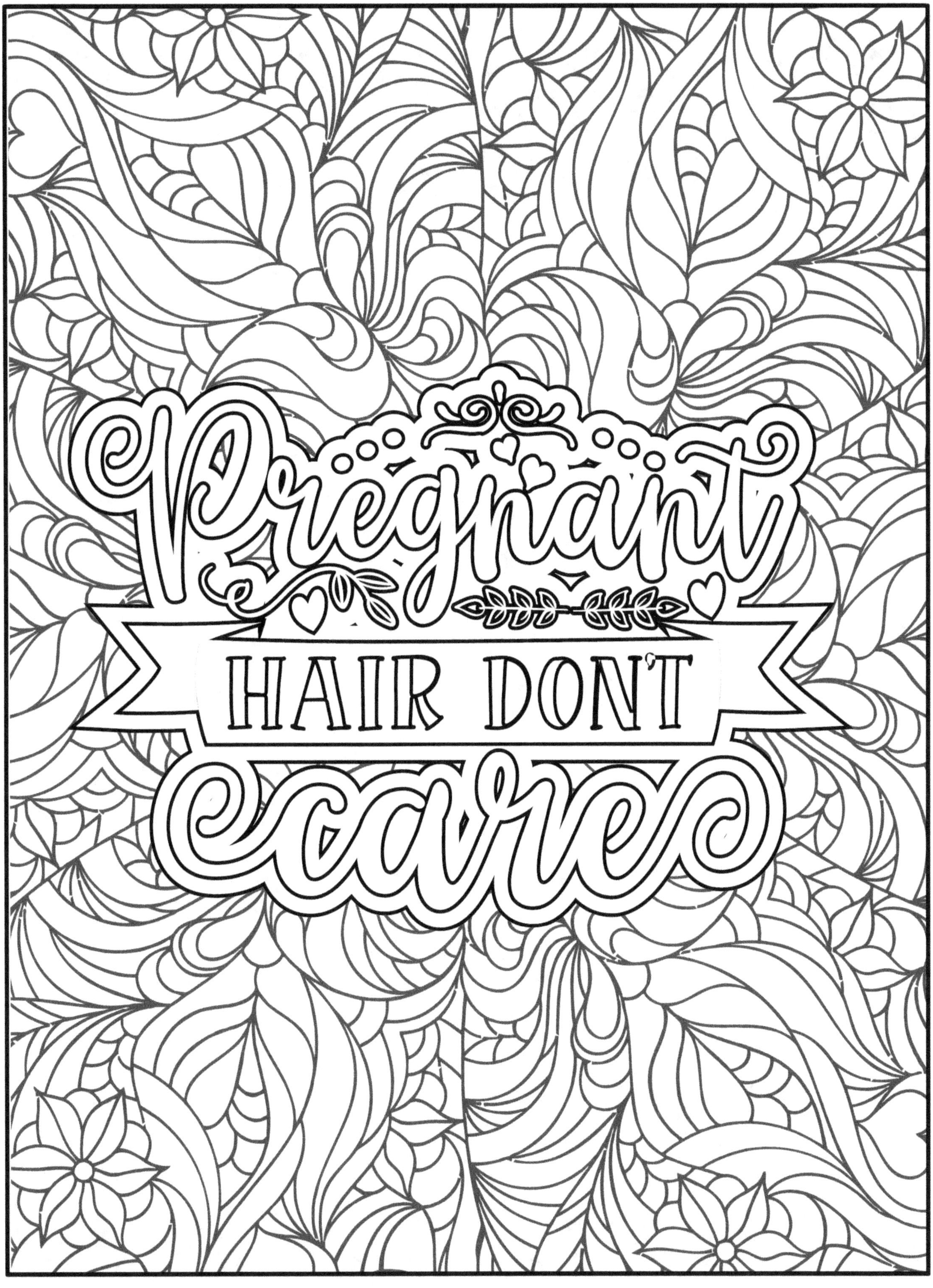
Pregnant
HAIR DON'T
care

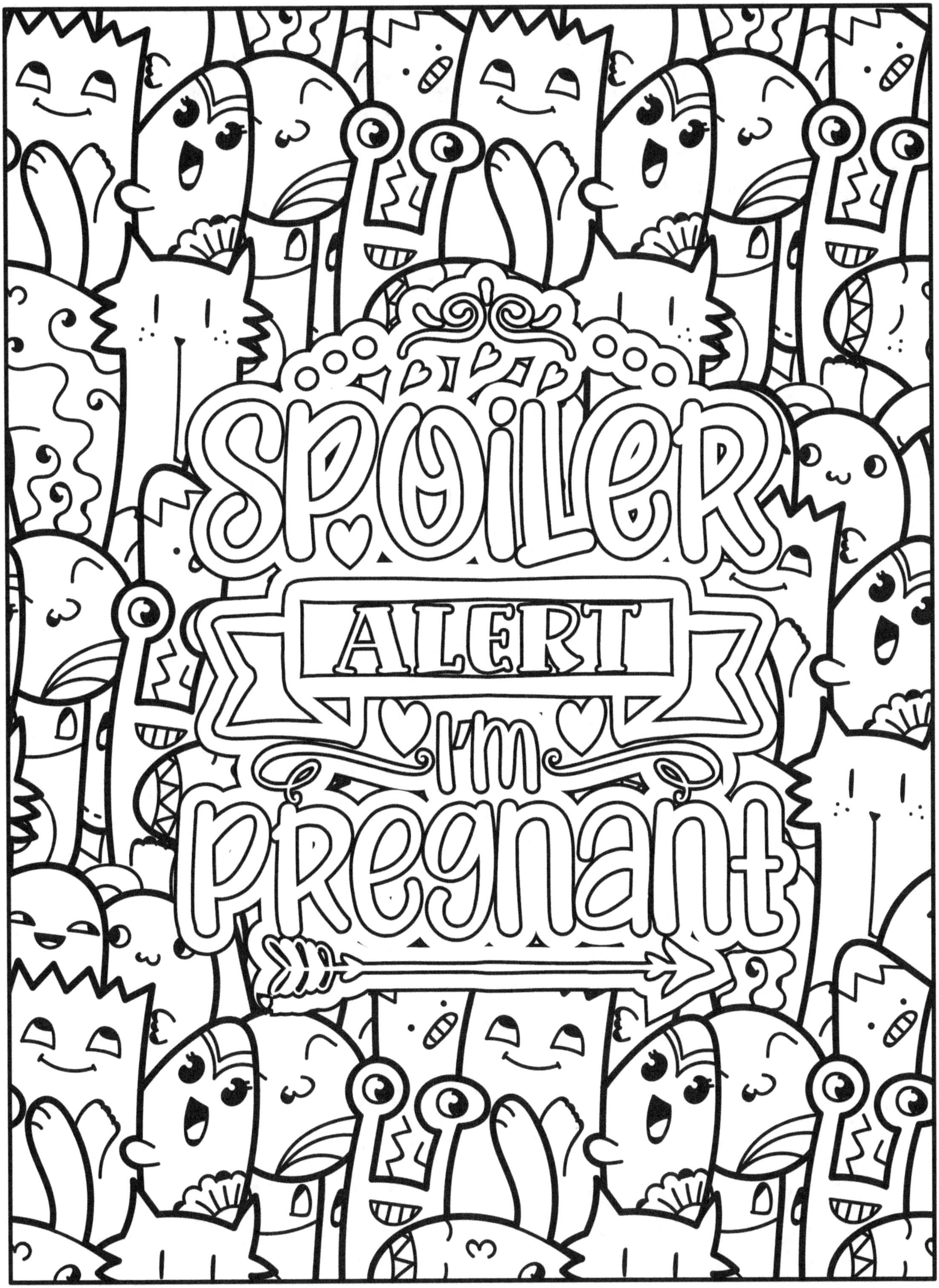
Spoiler
ALERT
I'm
Pregnant

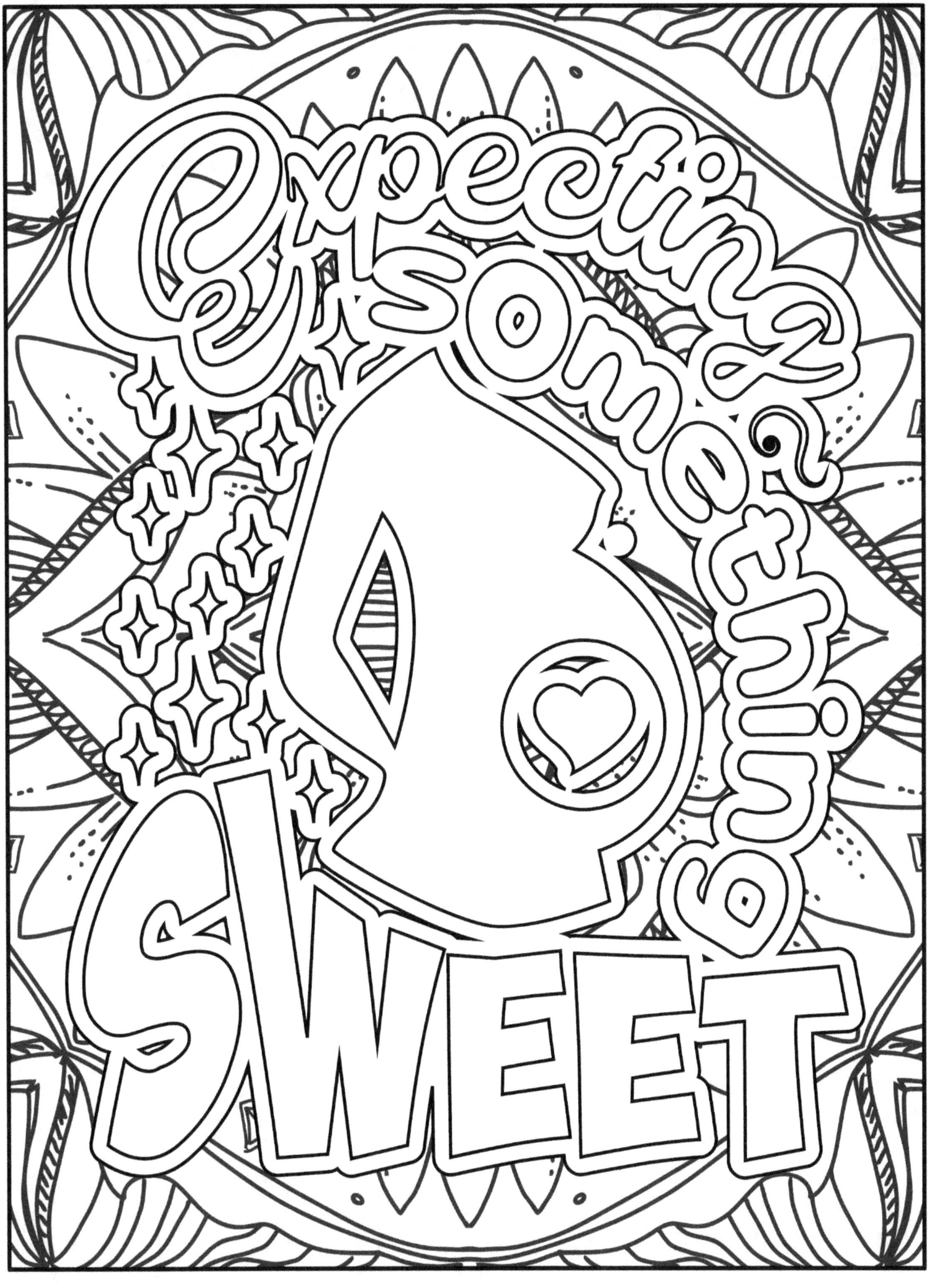
Expecting
something
SWEET

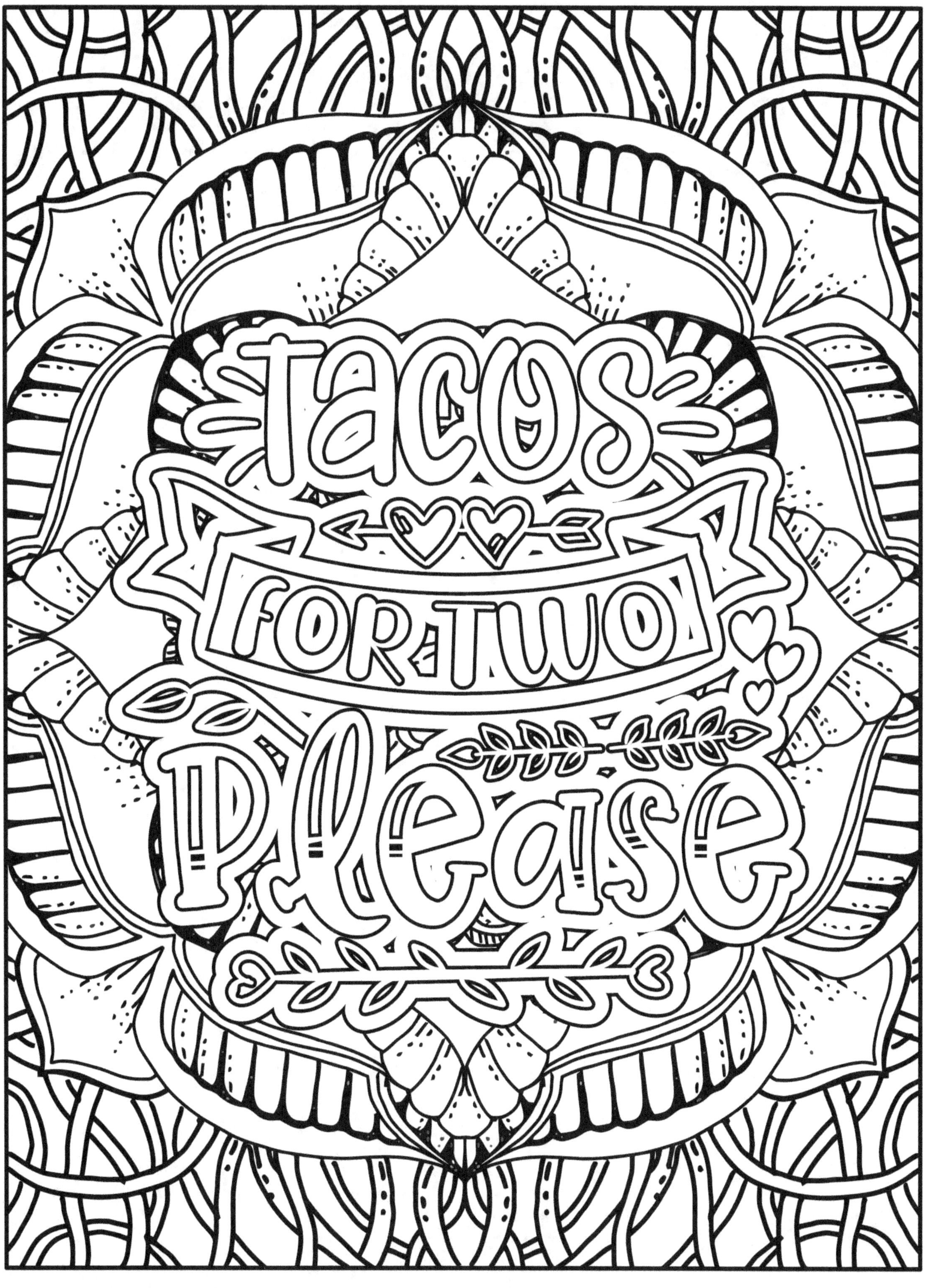
Tacos
For Two
Please

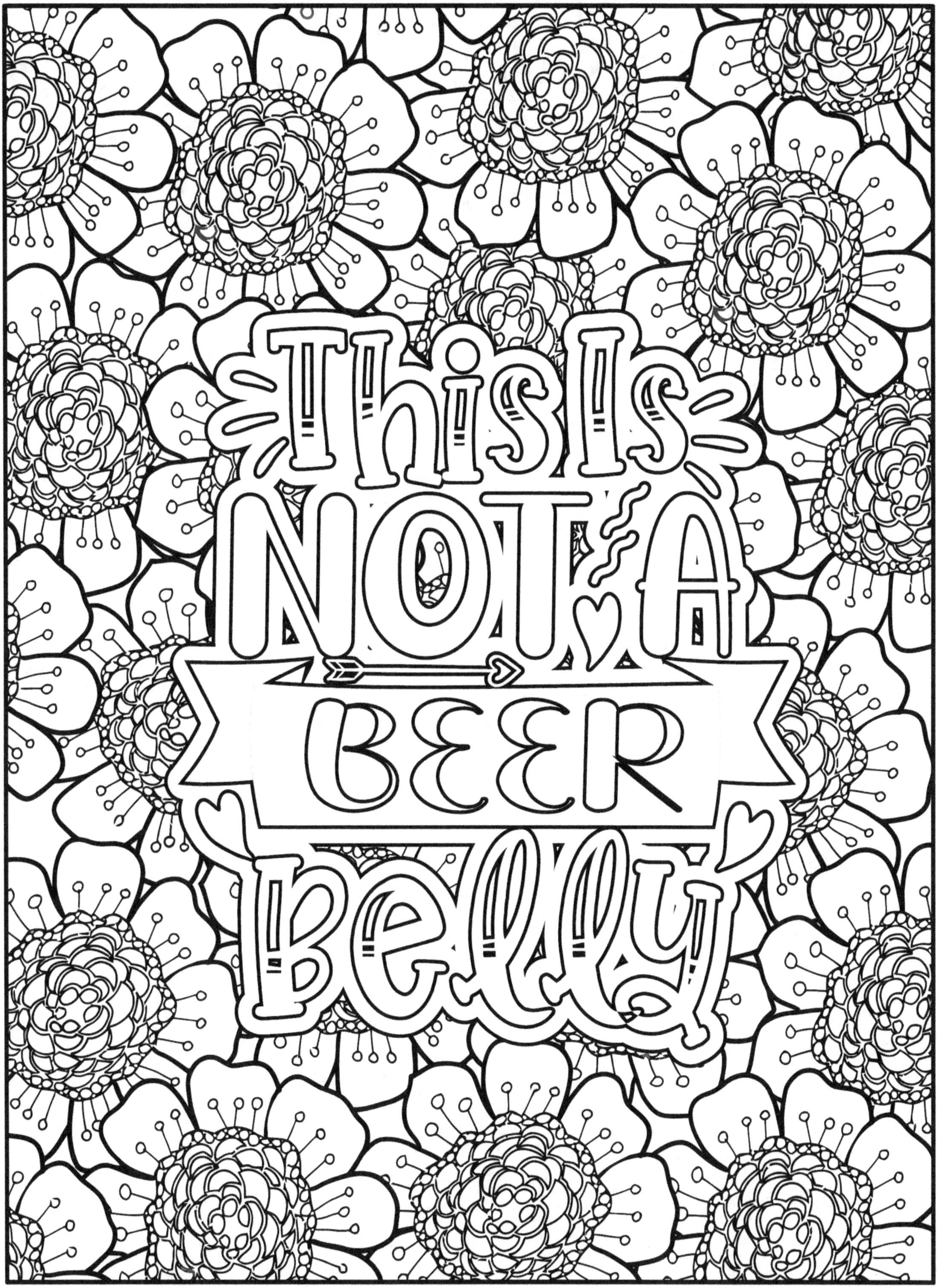
This Is
NOT A
BEER
Belly

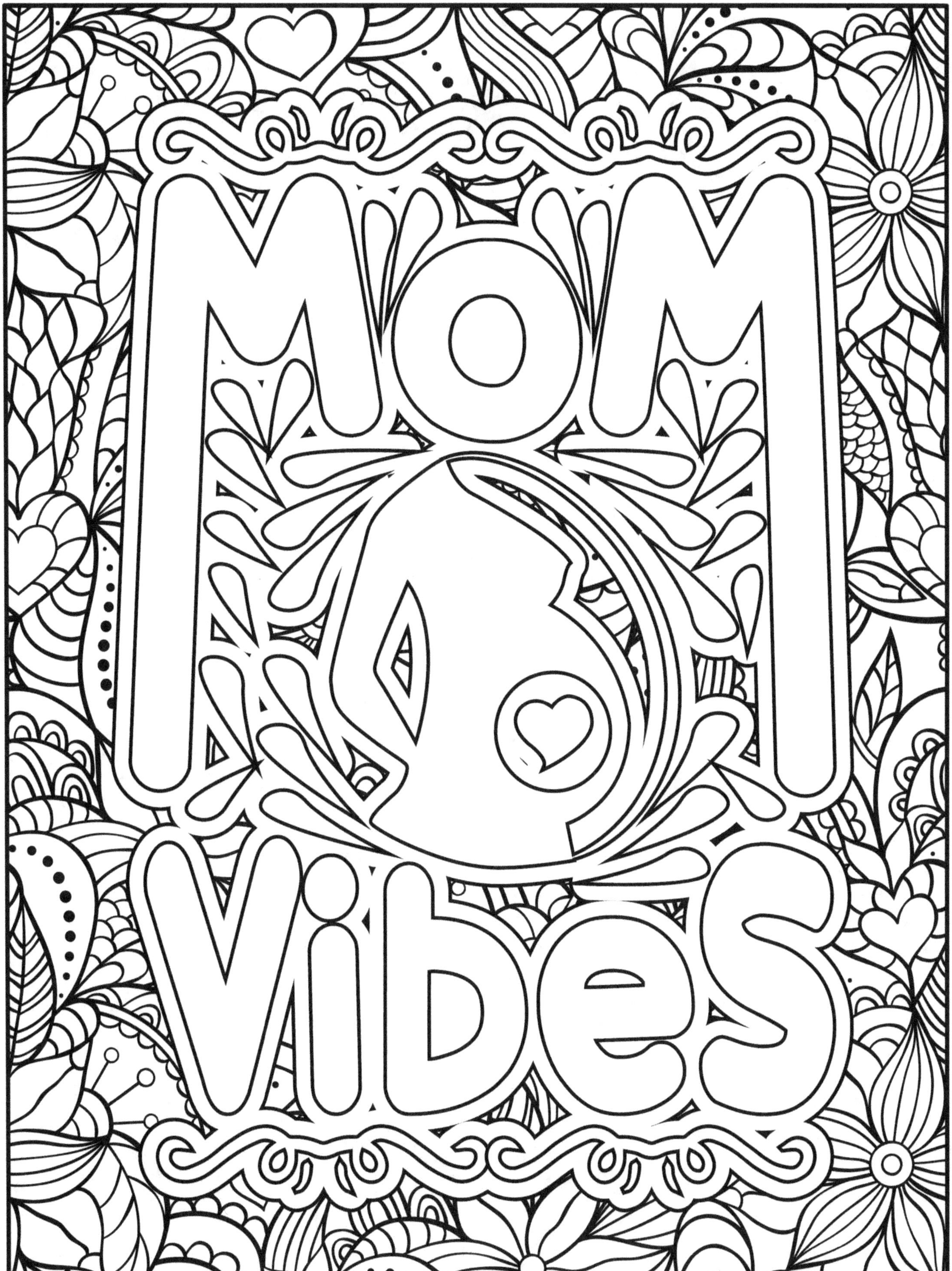
MOM
VIBES

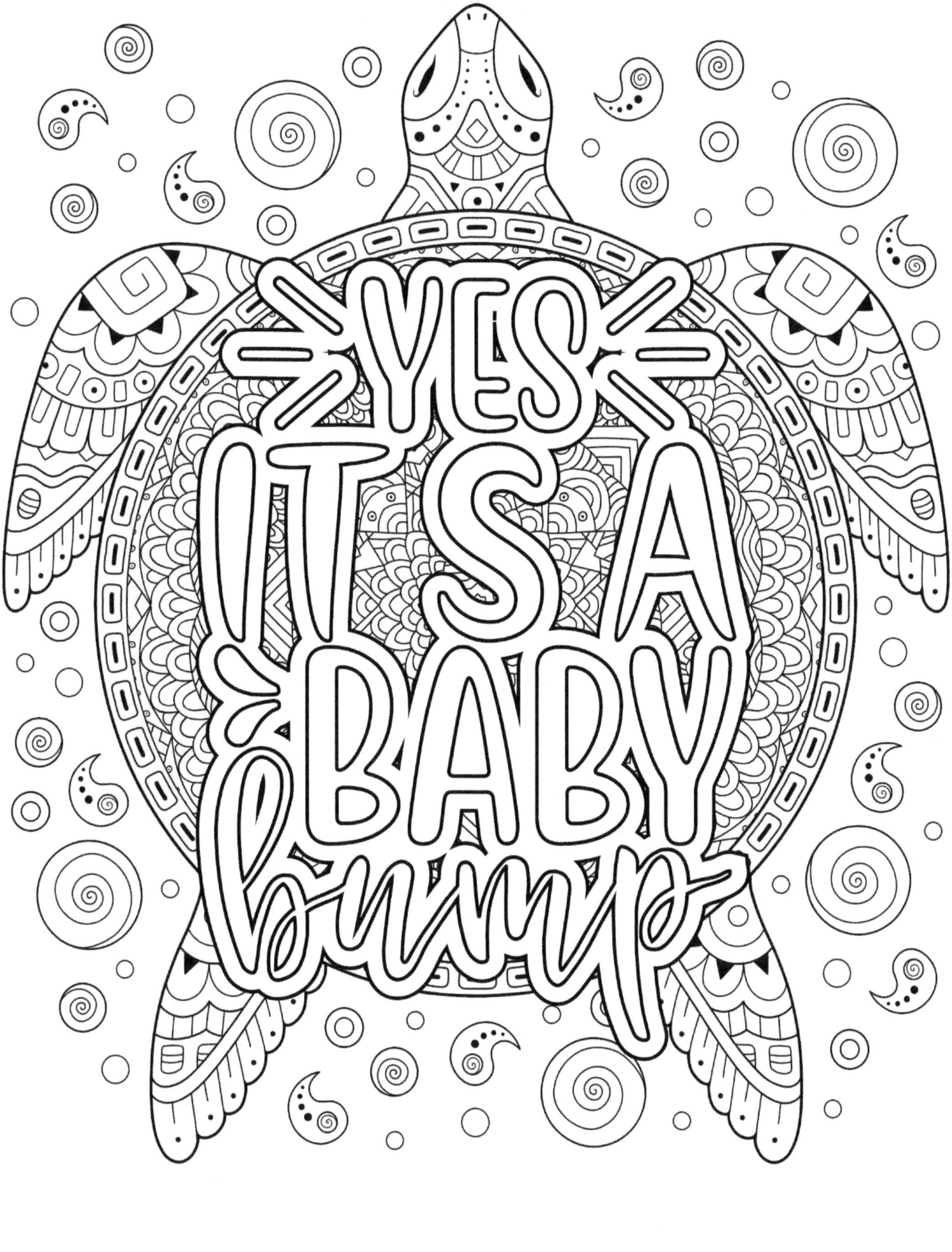
YES
IT'S A
BABY
bump

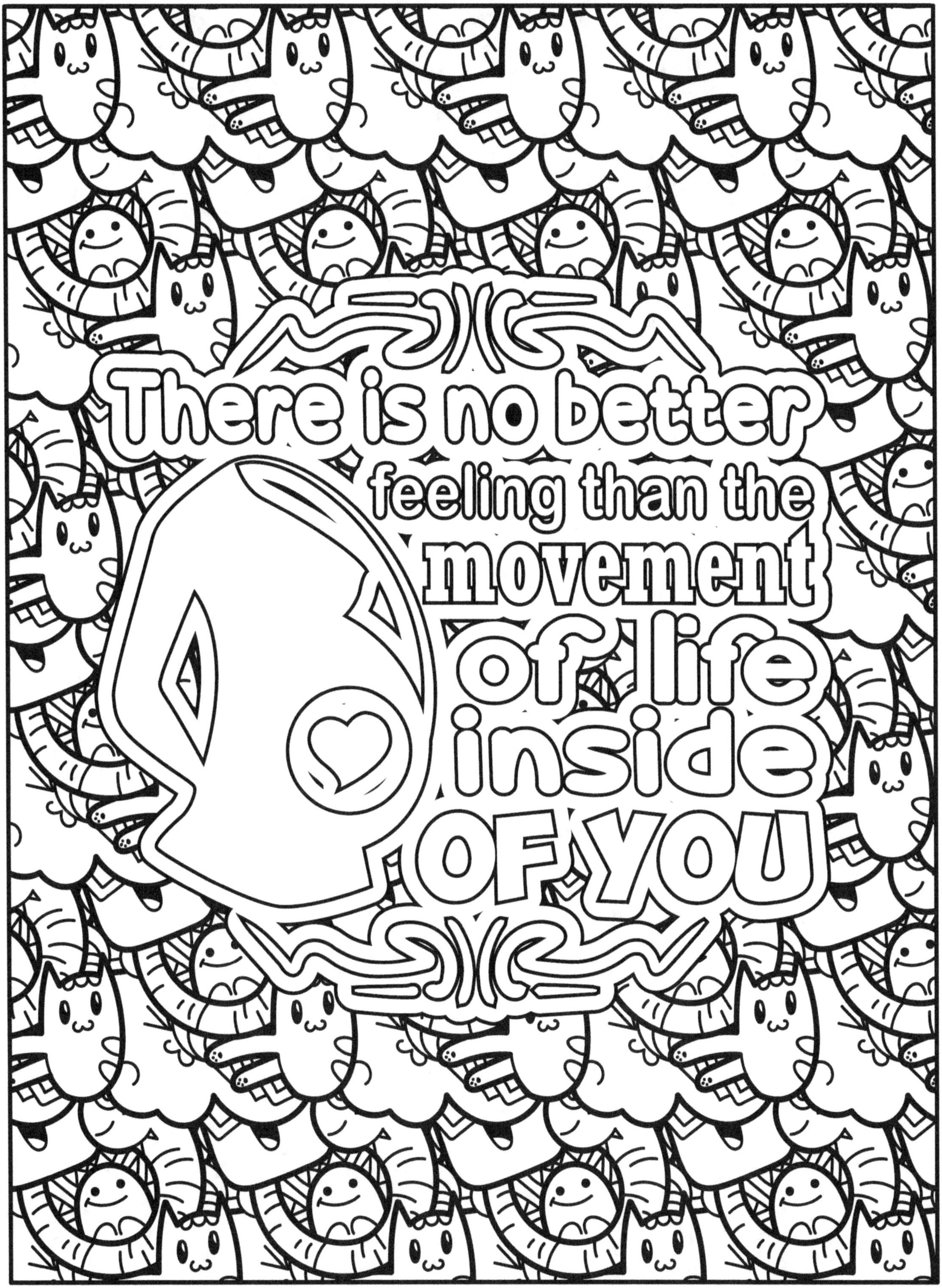
There is no better
feeling than the
movement
of life
inside
OF YOU

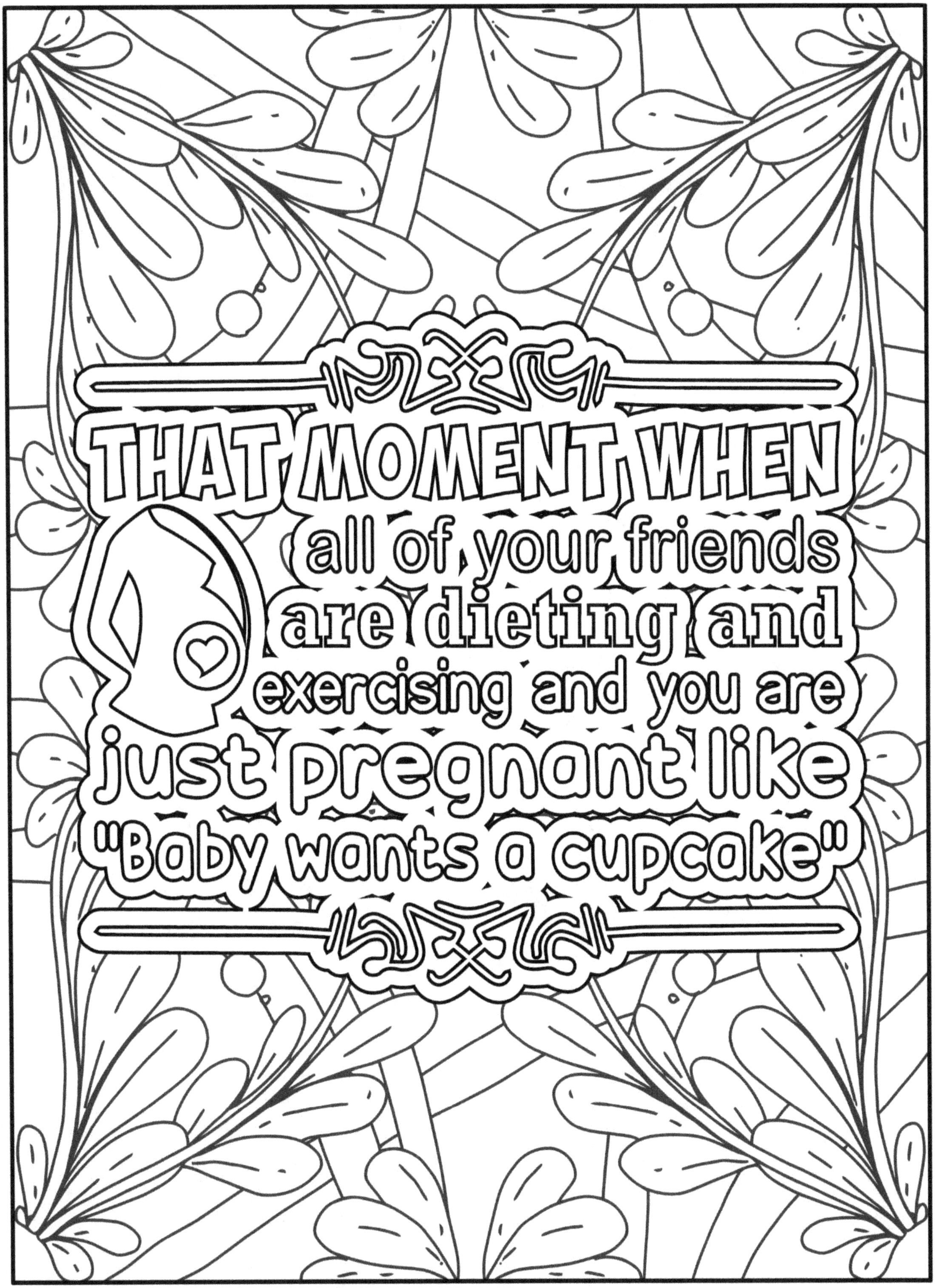
THAT MOMENT WHEN
all of your friends
are dieting and
exercising and you are
just pregnant like
"Baby wants a cupcake"

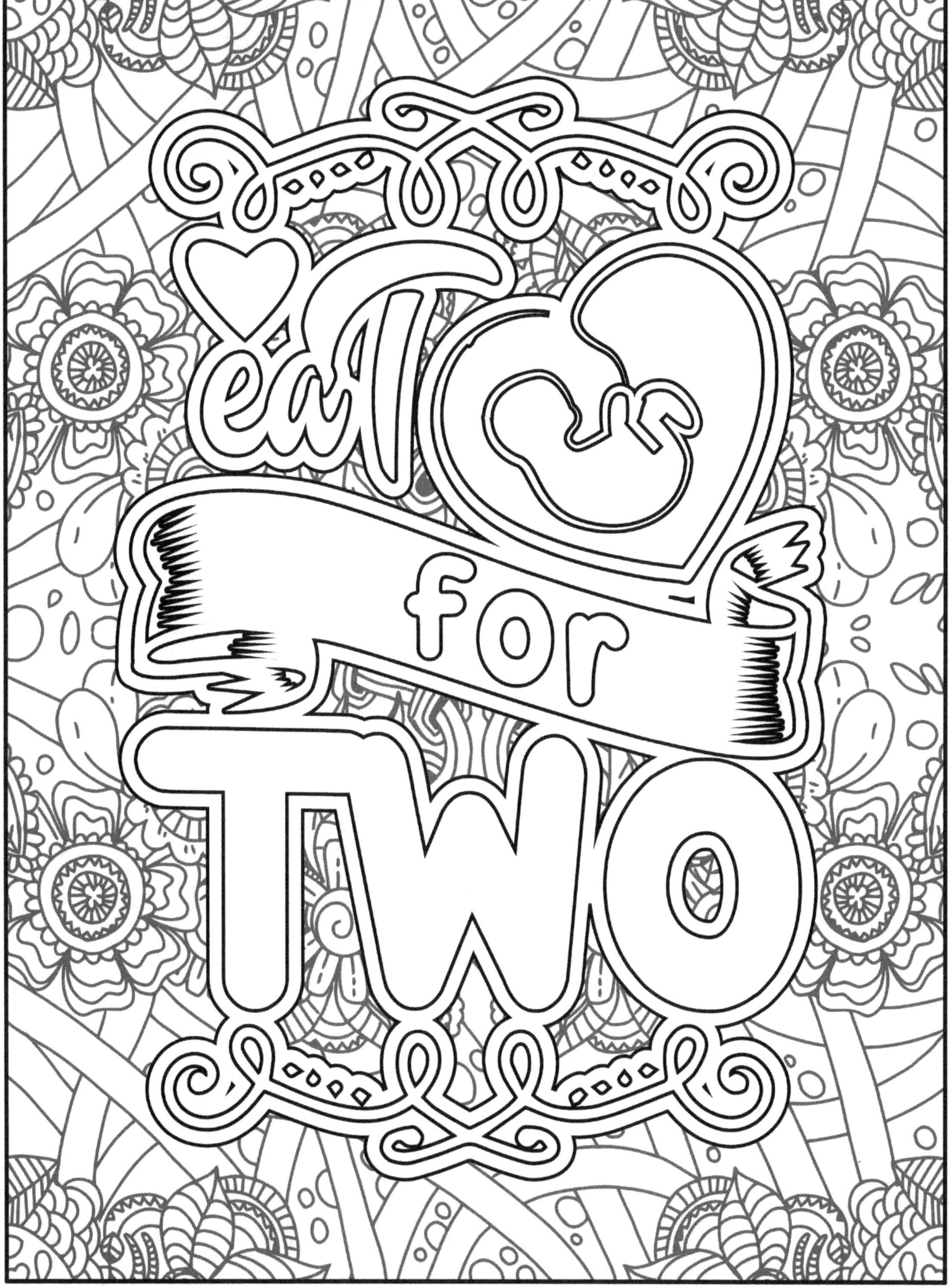
eat
for
TWO

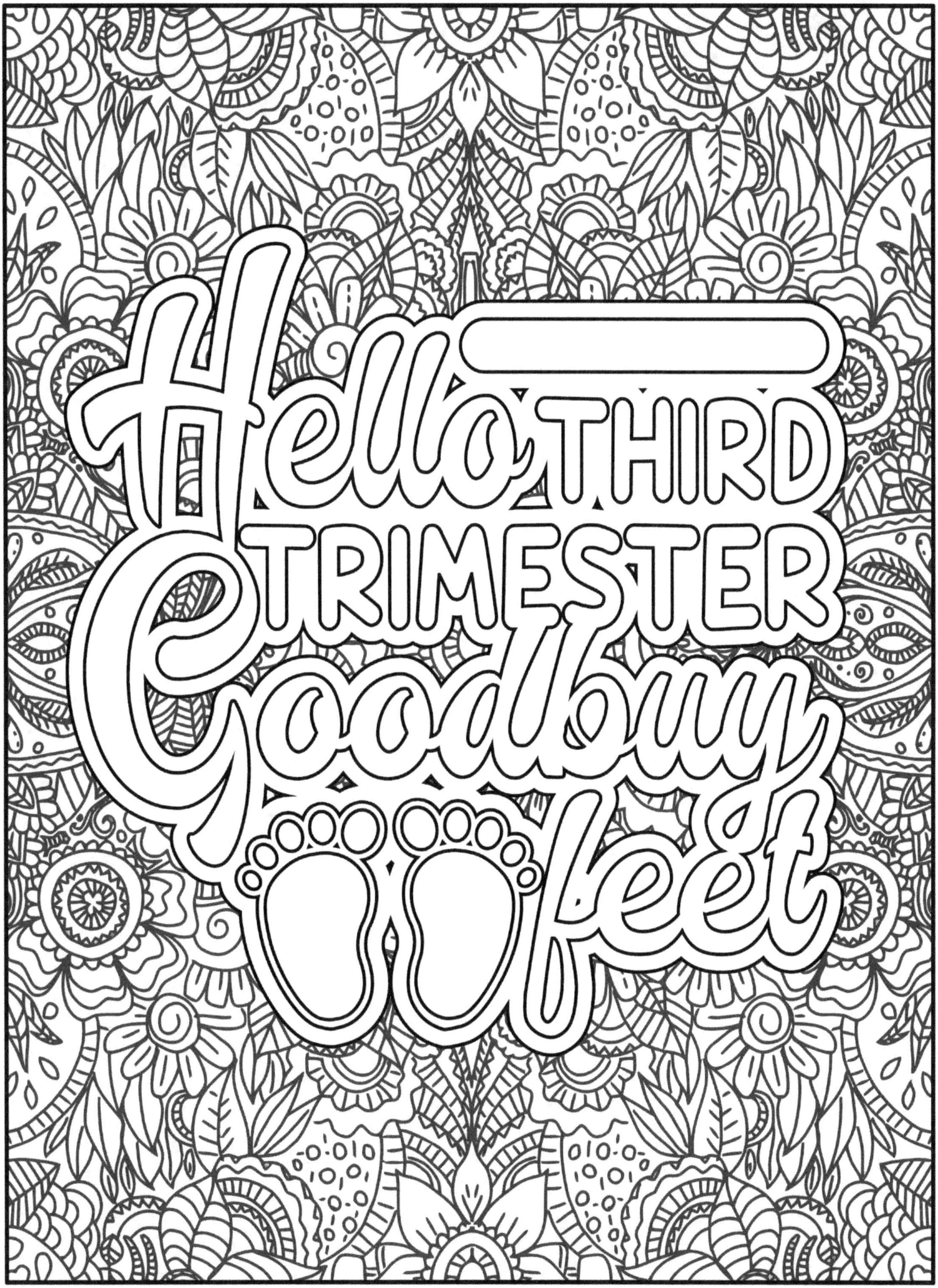
Hello THIRD
TRIMESTER
Goodbuy
feet

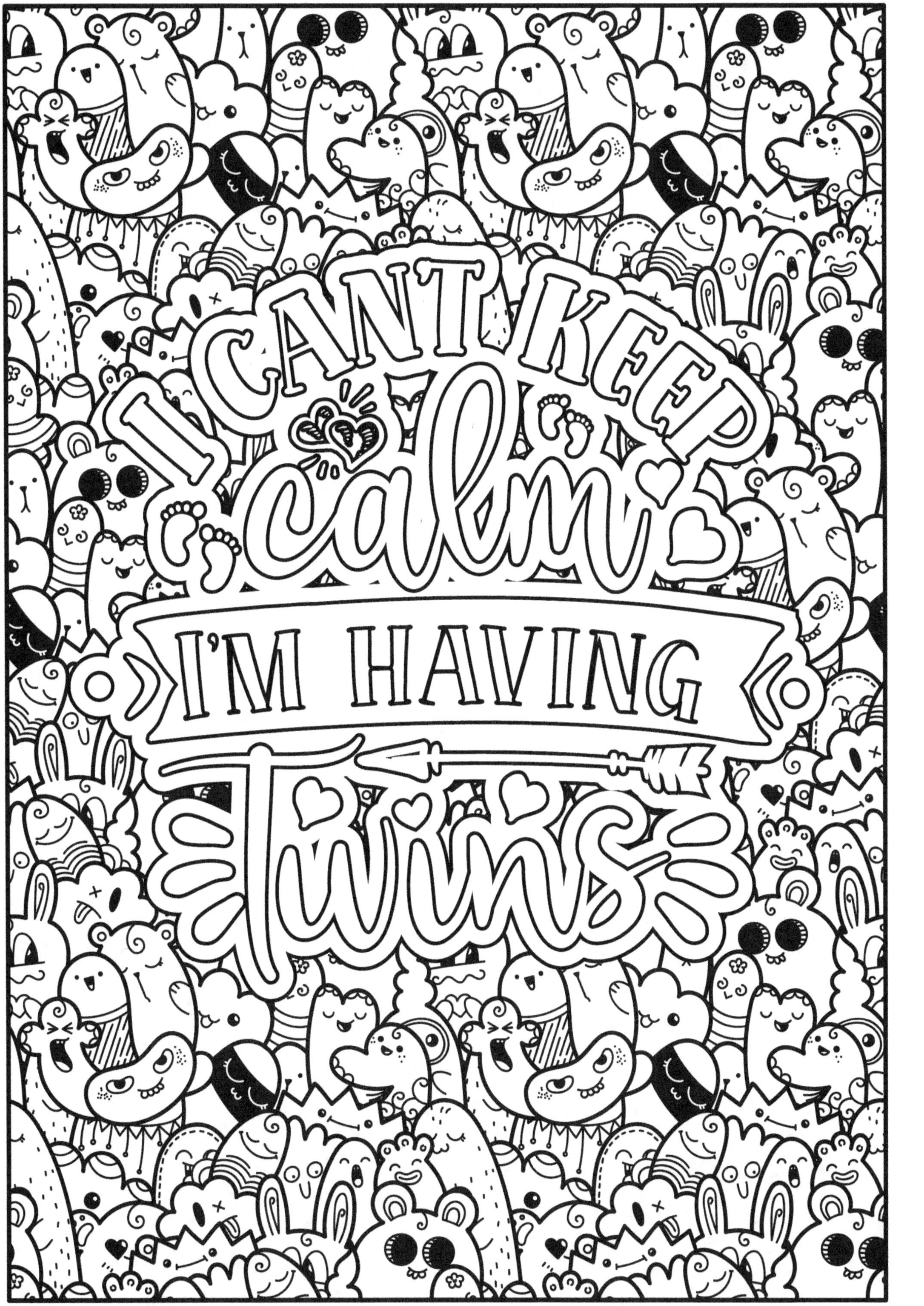
I CANT KEEP calm
I'M HAVING
Twins

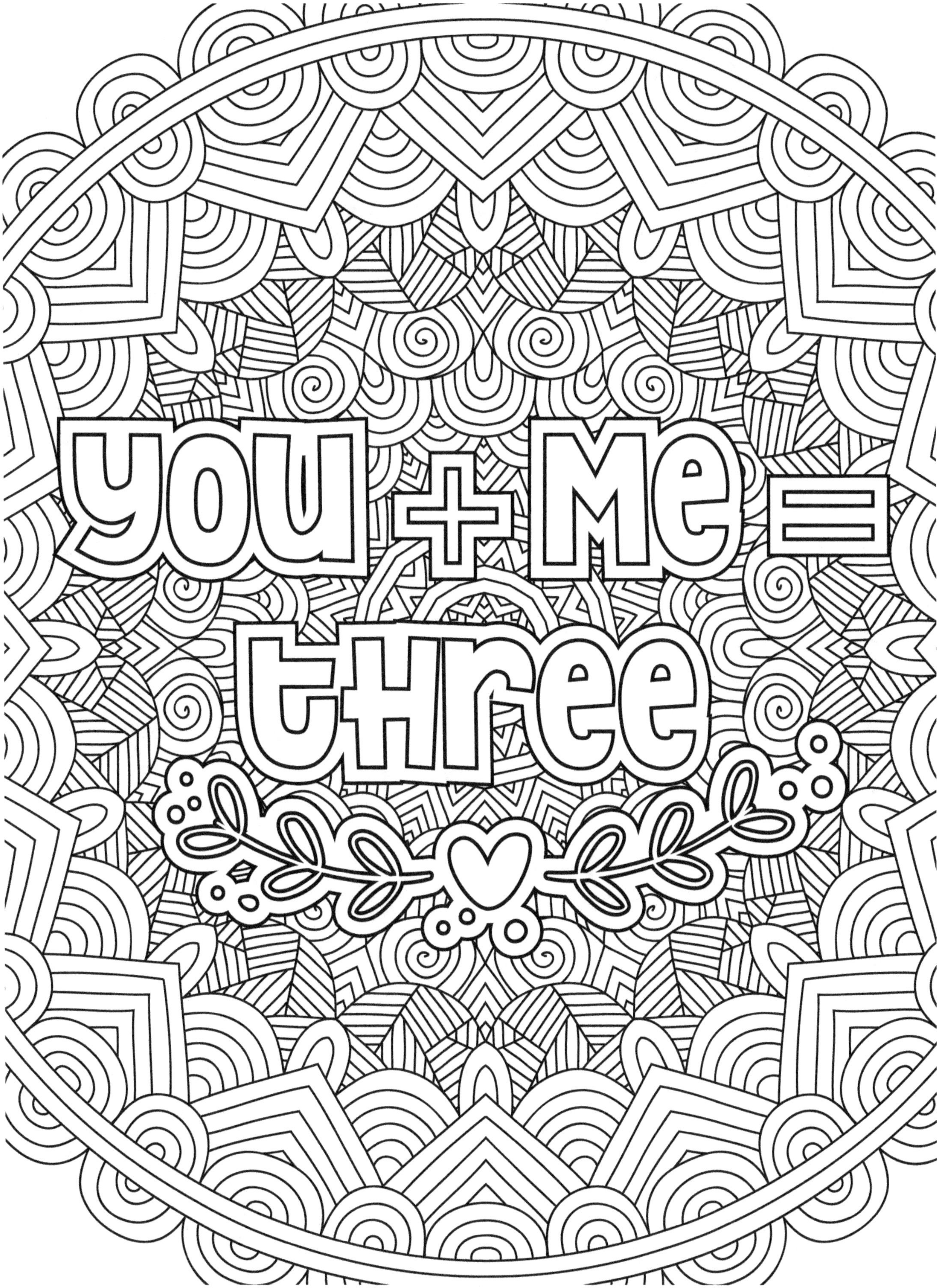
you + me =
three

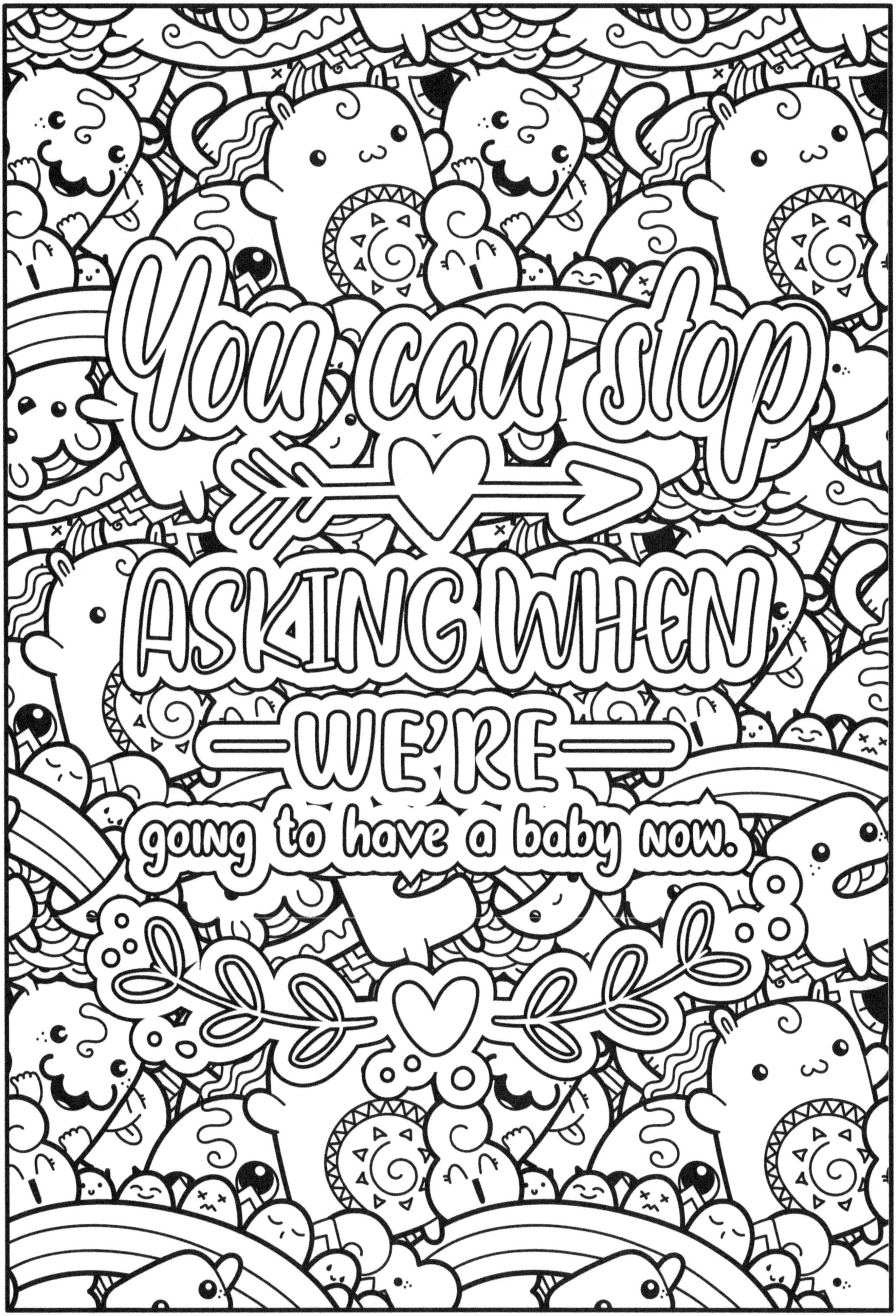
You can stop
ASKING WHEN
WE'RE
going to have a baby now.